MAKING IT
IT
BIG
IN
AMERICA

MAKING IT BIG IN AMERICA

ANDREW WOOD

Prima Publishing
Rocklin, California

© 1995 by Andrew Wood

Library of Congress Cataloging-in-Publication Data
Wood, Andrew.
    Making it big in America : a self-made millionaire tells how anyone can get ahead in business and life / Andrew Wood.
      p. cm.
    ISBN 0-7615-0018-9
    1. Success in business—United States. 2. Entrepreneurship—United States. 3. Success—United States. I. Title.
HF5386.W838   1993
650.1—dc20   95-3304
                                                CIP

95 96 97 98 99 AA 10 9 8 7 6 5 4 3 2

Printed in the United States of America

How to Order:
Single copies may be ordered from Prima Publishing, P.O. Box 1260BK, Rocklin, CA 95677; telephone (916) 632-4400. Quantity discounts are also available. On your letterhead, include information concerning the intended use of the books and the number of books you wish to purchase.

DEDICATION

This book is dedicated to all those who played a part in my making it big in America: My mother and father; Lennored and Ginger Theberge; J. J. and Mary Anne Wurthner; the guy who gave me a lift in a Ford Pinto from Washington to West Palm Beach; Dick Pearce; Brad from Boston and Sandra from Glasgow from our days at Jason's Yogurt store, wherever you are; Pat McCary; Dennis Wojakouski; Rob Talbot; John Fennel; Raymond; David Gardner; Dean Moss; Jim from Atlantis CC; Kiser Khan; Cambell Bouge; the Springers; the Cooks; Fred; Stev; Ron Krenz; Frank Elkins; Jim Holzer; David and Terry Miller; Peter Brusso; Tony Vercillo; Dave Cater; Mike Noad; Ruth and Jim Lowry, and my wife Sue, who has been there through the hard times; and all the others I should thank whose names elude me at the moment.

CONTENTS

Lesson Six: Getting the Most Important Person in the World to Help You

Lesson Seven: How to Market Yourself

PREFACE

I was born in Oxford, England. At the age of eighteen I came to America on vacation. Within a few hours of arriving I decided I did not want to go back to Europe. The lifestyles and opportunities America offered were just too appealing.

After working without pay at a golf club so that I could play for free I eventually got a walk-on golf scholarship at Palm Beach junior college. After three years I left school and, armed with nothing more than a burning desire to succeed, set off in search of the American Dream.

I moved to California to work as a chauffeur for a friend's limousine company. When I arrived I found a business that although it was only five months old was on its last legs. Although the two owners could afford to pay cash for two limousines, they had no sense of how to run a business: They had no business cards and no advertising, and they seldom answered the phone. In fact, the business had already lost $80,000 before my first day on the job! The owners had no desire to lose any more money. So, within two weeks of my arrival, they decided to shut the business down.

That left me with no job, with nowhere to stay, and with no money.

But just five years later, at the age of twenty-nine, things had changed dramatically for me: I had become a millionaire! America is truly the land of opportunity—where else can you start with nothing and become a millionaire in just a few years?

If I can make it big in America, so can you. In this book I will let you in on many of the missing links—the things that they never taught you in school—about making it big in life, about getting ahead and living to your full potential, and about success itself. This is not a get-rich quick book, although that may be exactly what happens if

you follow through on the principles it details. The keys to
success are not hard to find if you know where to look for
them. This book is the perfect place to start.

All the best,
Andrew Wood

INTRODUCTION

I listened to a great many audio tapes, read books, and watched videos on how to improve my life. They all had something good to say but none held the solution to the puzzle of success. This book does.

This book will teach you what you need to know to start with nothing and succeed in America. It will show you how to get the most out of your life. If you already have a job, money, and a decent lifestyle, then so much the better! You will learn how to maximize your efforts. If you are stuck in a rut, unhappy with your job, or just plain bored then you have picked up the right book. Follow what I have to say and you will find a new sense of enthusiasm spurring you on.

I hope you will get a great many good ideas from this book. But even if you only get a few, your time and money will have been well spent. One good idea can go a long way in helping you reach the top. Perhaps some of the ideas presented here may be familiar to you, but I will bet you have not yet put them into practice. If this program helps you to do that, then you will have invested wisely.

While many of the principles I present are simple, that does not make them any less a piece of the puzzle of success. Put all these simple ideas together and you will have a powerful formula for success in business and in your personal life.

If you read this book only once, you will not do justice to it or to yourself. It is full of ideas and strategies. These ideas will spark your imagination, sending it off on tangents that in turn will lead you to generate your own good ideas. By returning to this book frequently you will pick up valuable insights you had previously overlooked. It's like an intricate movie that you must see several times to understand it fully. I promise it will reward you whenever you read it.

Let me give you some tips on how to benefit fully from your reading. First, read through the book completely once in order to get an overview. Then go back and read it again, one lesson at a time. Don't be afraid to take notes and plan your strategy for success. You are worth whatever time it takes.

When you have finished your second reading, go back through your notes and number each idea you will implement. After numbering your ideas, place another number alongside each idea to prioritized it based on its overall importance in your success strategy.

Finally, develop a schedule that will cover the next few months. Set specific dates for starting your plan for success. Pick a day each week to review your goals and to refine your schedule and strategies where necessary. By working in this fashion you will stay on track, never straying far from your path to success.

The concepts presented here work. I know, they made me a millionaire. And they will work for you, too. But you must apply them. It's an unfortunate fact that only 5 percent of the people who read this book will ultimately implement the steps necessary for success. But they will be the ones who quickly rise to the top of their respective professions and live the lives of their dreams. Will you be one of them? The choice is up to you.

LESSON 1

BREAKING THROUGH YOUR MENTAL BARRIERS

WHY MOST PEOPLE FAIL TO ACHIEVE SUCCESS

It's no secret that few people live life up to their full potential. Unfortunately, most people either never get close to living the lives they dream of or else rise quickly to a certain level and then grind to a halt, stuck in a rut. How can you avoid becoming one of the statistics? How can you get an edge in business and in life to ensure that your life becomes everything you always hoped it would? Surprisingly, the answer is simple.

Have you heard of the old business principle KISS? You know, "Keep It Simple, Stupid"? Well, simple things work, that is a fact. The things that work best are always simple because the more complicated a solution is the more chance it has to go wrong. Real success comes from putting all the small, simple things together into a system. If you faithfully do that, you will find yourself far ahead of the pack.

One of the first things to do on your quest for success is to thoroughly understand why so few people actually succeed. There are twelve simple skills that spell the difference between those at the top and those who fail. Some people fail in just one category. Others, however, get very creative and mix a combination of these twelve reasons into a sure-fire plan for disaster.

Read the following list of reasons carefully and ask yourself if any or all of them apply to you.

Twelve Reasons Few People Get What They Want out of Life

1. They impose mental limitations on themselves as to what they can achieve.
2. They feel they are not lucky.
3. They have no clear path of where they want to go or what they want from life.
4. They fail to develop a written strategy.
5. They do not invest in themselves.
6. They never learn to get others to help them.
7. They do not market themselves.
8. They do not know how to sell themselves.
9. They do not solve their problems well.
10. They lack motivation.
11. They fail to take action.
12. They lack persistence.

Do some of these reasons apply to you? If so, don't worry. We will have a separate lesson to examine each and to show you how to conquer each problem with simple methods that have proven to be effective.

A few simple words, phrases, actions, attitudes, and decisions can make a huge difference in whether a person is successful, mediocre, or a total failure. Most people never learn what these simple things are. Let us take a look at the main reasons people fail to live up to their potential and see what can be done to change this.

THE FEAR OF SUCCESS

A great many people fail to make it big because the thought of making it big scares them to their very core. Making it big means having more money, more responsibility, more chance of failure, and more pressure.

Let's take these fears one at a time and look closely at each.

Fear of Money

Many people unconsciously associate money with the negative things in life. Although they would argue vigorously that this is not true of them—that they would love being rich—they would then proceed to bombard you with a host of popular misconceptions like these.

Misconceptions about People with Money

- People with money are selfish.
- People with money step on others to get ahead.
- People with money are snobs.
- People with money are bad or evil.
- People with money can't be trusted.

With negative thoughts like these echoing throughout our society is it any wonder that many people subconsciously don't want to have money? They simply do not want to be associated with these negative misconceptions.

The fact is people with money are no better or worse, as people, than those without money. They do of course have more resources at their disposal to help others should they wish to, and so will you when you realize your true potential. Then it is up to you to decide what you do with your money. You can use it to help others and for good causes or you can choose to keep it for yourself. The choice is yours.

It is like the old saying "Guns don't kill people; people kill people." Well, money itself is neither good nor bad. It is the people who use it who determine if it is put to a good use or a poor one. If you had unlimited resources and not a care in the world would you help others with your wealth or would you look for ways to hurt others? Of course you would do good and so do a vast majority of those who already have a great deal of money. They donate billions of dollars a year to help churches, museums, hospitals, art galleries, research, and relief organizations.

As I have already said many people do not realize that they fear having money. It is buried deep down in their subconscious and only surfaces now and then to sabotage any endeavor that might lead to great wealth.

To remove any fears you may have about money start right now by thinking of all the good and positive ways you can help those in your community, state, and country. Think about those who need help the most and think of how you will use your money to help them when you make it big.

There are many other popular sayings besides those about people that help many people to be afraid of making money.

Are These Age-Old Gems
Limiting Your Success?

- Money doesn't grow on trees so hold on to it for all it's worth. Don't ever risk it in a venture that might pay off big.

- Getting rich is hard work. It's not worth killing yourself for. (Of course it's not worth killing yourself for, but people with great financial resources usually don't. In fact they often live longer because they have more interests and more goals to strive after. They have more time to exercise, take more vacations, eat the best foods, live in the best places, and have access to the best medical care in the country. It's a tough life, but someone has to live it!)
- The best things in life are free. (True. But the second best things cost plenty! So if you intend to enjoy them you'd better include making lots of money in your plans.)

Someone once asked the actor Michael Caine if money had made him happy. He replied: "I have been rich and unhappy. I have been poor and unhappy, and it was a lot nicer when I was rich and unhappy."

If you have negative feelings about money write them down now in the spaces below. Then write down next to each negative thought all the good things you can do to help yourself, family, friends, and others when you have the money and resources to do so. You will soon see that the positive things you can do with money will always outweigh your negative feelings.

My Negative Feelings about Money Are

1. _____
2. _____
3. _____
4. _____
5. _____

Dudley Moore, who played the billionaire in the movie *Arthur,* summed it up best. When asked by a shopkeeper how it felt to have all that money, his face lit up in a smile and he simply said, "It's great!" And it is, so don't let negative thoughts about money hold you back.

> Resolve now to leave all negative concepts of money behind you. Money is good if you use it for good. When you make it big you will use your money to do good.

Fear of Responsibility

Another fear that you must overcome in order to start off on the road to success is the fear of responsibility. Some people hate to take on more responsibility; they think it means more hassles and more stress. They already have families to care for, they reason. If they make it big, then they must add to their list of concerns employees, accountants, lawyers, and stockbrokers. Others would place demands on their time. They couldn't get by with just punching the clock like their friends. And to a degree they are right: It does take extra effort to make it big. So, instead, they choose to languish in the pools of mediocrity.

What negative feelings do you have about taking on more responsibility? Write down any negative feelings you have, then offset them with positives like more respect from your peers, more money, and more vacation time.

My Negative Feelings about Responsibility Are

1. _____
2. _____
3. _____
4. _____
5. _____

Fear of Failure

The fear of failure is the granddaddy of all fears to be over-come before making it big. I will talk more about this more later, but for right now you must realize that being suc-cessful also means risking failure. It means leaving your comfort zone, and it means ignoring pressure from your parents, spouse, and friends and taking a bold step forward in pursuit of your dreams. Many of the greatest success stories have risen out of the ashes of failure.

It all depends on how you look at failure. If you view failure as the end of the story, then it will be. If, like Thomas Edison, you look at every failure as another suc-cess because it shows you how not to achieve your goals, you will continue on in pursuit of greatness.

It is this simple optimistic outlook that very often is the deciding factor in whether people make it big. Telling yourself that you have failed will result in negative thoughts, emotions, and future actions. Telling yourself that because of this failure you have learned and will therefore build success will create a much different mind-set and attitude. I call this change of attitude *Reframing*. I will talk more about this process in the lesson on moti-vation. For now realize that past failures mean nothing. They are gone and can't be replayed. Concern yourself only with the future. You start each new day with a clean slate and it's up to you what you do with that day. Will you use it to create a new and exciting future for yourself or will you use it to dwell on the past? It's up to you.

I Am Afraid of Failure Because

1. _____
2. _____
3. _____
4. _____
5. _____

Some people are not only afraid of failure, but they are also afraid of success. You may find this hard to believe, but think about it. I'll bet you can instantly call to mind several people you know who have absolutely no interest in being any better off than they are now. Sure, they might say they want to make more money or get a new car but all they are doing is paying lip service to improving their situation. They have no idea how to make this happen, instead they talk in terms of wishes: "I wish I had a million dollars!" or "I wish I could vacation in Fiji!" The actual thought of turning these wishes into reality, however, is simply too overwhelming for them to comprehend. In short they wish for things because they do not ever expect to have them. The fear of success scares them so much that they can't even get off the couch. These people have a combination of all the other fears rolled into one. They never expected to achieve anything in their life and so even if success were handed to them on a plate they would be forced to turn it down.

Fear of Guilt

Some people achieve a reasonable level of success in their life and then begin to feel guilty about it. They ask themselves questions like "Why am I so lucky when there are so many homeless people?" or "Should I really buy a new Jaguar when there are people starving in Africa?" Or perhaps they feel guilty because they have attained a level of success beyond that of their family or friends. Slowly but surely they destroy what success they have with their guilt. This is sad because there is no reason to feel guilty about success. One of the most rewarding things that success brings is the means to help those who are less fortunate. The more successful you are, the more resources you will have, and with more resources you can help more people. And if you are helping others, is there any reason to feel guilty?

Fear of Change

Humans are unique among the animals in that they can adapt to just about anything provided the change is made slowly. But ask them to change rapidly or on a large scale and they will have a problem. They will be forced to leave their comfort zone, break habits and adopt new ones, and generally do things differently than before. Since change involves risk and unknown outcomes, it makes many people feel insecure. So instead of making any changes, they stay stuck in whatever rut or comfort zone they find themselves in at the moment, never fulfilling their true potential.

My Negative Feelings about Making Changes Are

1. _____
2. _____
3. _____
4. _____
5. _____

SUCCESS PLAYS NO FAVORITES

Many people kill their chances of reaching their full potential by giving themselves excuses. Despite what you might have heard, success is beyond the reach of no one. I know this is true because there are literally thousands of shining examples of success from every age group, ethnic background, and educational standing.

Steven Jobs, the cofounder of Apple Computer, was a billionaire at age twenty-nine, having started with a small business in his garage. Colonel Sanders, the founder of Kentucky Fried Chicken, started his business when he was sixty-six years old. He did not become very wealthy until well into his seventies.

Many people feel that they are undereducated and should wait until they have some kind of degree before they embark on their mission to success. This too is a falsehood. Many of the people on the Forbes 400, the annual survey of the 400 richest people in America, do not have a college degree. Several did not even get a high school diploma. Education is very important, but do not confuse textbook college courses with the type of education that will truly give you a head start in life.

Others make excuses because of their health, yet many people achieve success despite seemingly insurmountable handicaps. People such as Stevie Wonder and Ray Charles became world famous musicians despite blindness. They are also good examples of how success knows no color or creed. Although even in this day and age some people may have to work harder than others because of prejudice, nevertheless opportunities are still theirs for the making. Armed with the tools provided in this book any person, regardless of background, can achieve success.

THE BIGGEST OBSTACLE YOU WILL EVER ENCOUNTER

The first and most formidable obstacle you must face on the road to success is you. Success does not depend on your age, color, appearance, creed, luck, or any of the hundreds of other mythical factors you hear discussed daily in coffee shops and bars across the country. You see, success does not occur by accident.

Success in life depends on one thing and one thing alone—*You*. Now that's pretty scary, isn't it? But you are, quite simply, the person in control of your own destiny.

Whatever path in life you choose will be your free choice, for better or worse. There is no one to blame for failure or to praise for success but you. The Seventh Cavalry will not come charging across the hill to your rescue if things don't go as planned. Neither will Superman, or the knight in shinning armor on the white horse who used to save you as a child. It is all up to you and you alone.

President Harry Truman had a plaque on his desk in the White House that read "The Buck Stops Here." Make that your first resolve on your road to the top. Do not blame outside forces whenever things go wrong in your life. That's what people who don't succeed do. Face the facts: Somehow, whether through poor planning, lack of action, procrastination, or a thousand other reasons, the blame comes directly back to you.

Decide here and now that you are in charge of your own destiny and life. You do not need anyone else's permission to change your life. You do not have to plug away at a job you hate. You do not have to live in the same town or associate with the same people. If you feel you should be somewhere else or be doing something different, you can without asking anyone's permission. This is America; you can do whatever you want. The only person who has any power to stop you is you. Conquering your own mind is the first and biggest step in getting ahead in life.

Roger's Lesson: The Four-Minute Mile

In the spring of 1954 a young medical student at Oxford University entered a shoe shop in Wimbledon, near London, and asked the cobbler to make him a special pair of running shoes. He wanted them light and strong enough to last just twelve laps. The cobbler provided such a shoe and the young man improved them further by fitting them with special graphite spikes. These spikes gave him better traction than the metal ones commonly used because the graphite would slip more easily in and out of the cinder track on which he ran.

The young man knew that preparation and planning were key elements in reaching his goal, just as they are in any successful endeavor. They were, however, only part of the ingredients needed for what was soon to be known as the "Miracle Mile." The young man discovered that the hardest part of reaching his goal was not running the one-mile distance of the cinder track, it was conquering the six-inch space between his ears.

When Roger Bannister finally broke the four-minute mile on May 6th, 1954, people had been trying to run a mile in under four minutes for almost 2000 years. Since the time of the ancient games at the foot of Mount Olympus, runners had reached toward that seemingly impossible goal. Athletes had run in the Olympics, in international championships, and around the world yet no one at the highest level with gold medals and world records on the line had ever run a mile in less than four minutes. In fact, many of the coaches of Bannister's era actually believed that the attempt could well result in the death of the runner, thinking that the physical limits of human performance had been reached. If God wanted man to be faster, they reasoned, he would have given him four legs instead of two.

Nevertheless, within just a few weeks of Bannister's record-breaking run several others ran the mile in less than four minutes. How was this possible? Did the human race suddenly get faster in the summer of 1954?

Of course not. The answer is much simpler than that and it is your first key to making it big. The answer pure and simple is that there was a mental limitation on the part of the runners. Because no one else had ever done it, the world's greatest athletes either consciously or subconsciously did not believe that it could be done. In their minds they reasoned that man had simply met the limits of speed and endurance a few seconds short of the four-minute mile. Once this "fact" had been proven wrong, runners across the globe decided that if Roger Bannister could run a mile in four minutes, well, so could they.

If Bannister had looked at the record books or spoken to all those others who had tried before him, he would have simply given up his quest and never reached it. But he did not let other people's views or the supposed facts in the record books influence his resolve to succeed. He shed all limitations and went after his goal with a single-minded purpose that made him famous. In fact, his picture even graced the cover of the very first issue of *Sports Illustrated*.

I am sure you have experienced the very same phenomenon in one small way or another—I know I have. One vivid mental breakthrough I can remember was as a kid of fifteen playing golf. At the time I was playing three-and-a-half rounds a day—sixty-three holes. Although I ate, drank, and slept golf I could not shoot under par for any given nine holes. Almost every day I played nine holes in even par several times, but it seemed almost impossible to play just one shot better. This went on all summer.

Finally, one day at the end of summer, I was playing even par at the ninth hole when I missed the green and put my ball in a sand trap. I figured it was another disappointment. Then, out of nowhere, I holed my trap shot for a birdie to go one under par. From that day on I was able to play at least nine holes under par on a consistent basis.

CREATING YOUR OWN MIRACLES

Now it's your turn. Picture for a moment some of the mental barriers that once defeated you. What are some things that you have done that at one time just didn't seem possible?

- Have you lost weight or stopped smoking?
- Have you earned a degree or started your own business?
- Have you moved to another part of the country?

Remember the mental barriers that you have already conquered, no matter how small, and put that same power to work in your life to help you remove the bigger mental barriers to achieving success.

Once a mental barrier is conquered it becomes easy to do what formerly seemed impossible. But the greatest rewards go to those people who break their barriers before others do. Free your mind of its limitations. And if you feel you are lacking in some of the skills you need to achieve your goals, pick them up as you go along. The important thing is to break your mental barriers now!

When I was fourteen years old, I picked up a matchbox on which were written the words, "Someone is always doing what someone else said could not be done." Those words have stayed with me even to this day and I have repeated them regularly to those who said that something couldn't be done! Can you imagine how ridiculous it must have seemed to think of actually putting a man on the moon at the beginning of World War II, just thirty years before it was to become a reality? They were still using propeller-driven planes. Yet people dreamed that man could land on the moon, and so they set about trying to make that dream come true. They must have been ridiculed much the same as Columbus was when he suggested that if he sailed west he would not fall off the edge of the world because the world was round.

People by nature will always help you find excuses not to achieve more. They will always be ready to help you to erect new mental barriers and to reinforce the old ones. The reason is simple: it's human nature. You see, if you do too well it will make them look bad. And instead of risking that indignity they will counsel you to think hard about moving to the city because it's a cold and unfriendly place—besides, they will say, you grew up here in the country. They will encourage you to stay in a job you hate because you have invested so much time already, and maybe next year you will get the promotion you deserve. But what kind of investment is it if it gives you no pleasure and satisfaction in return?

Are you 100 percent happy with every aspect of your life right now?

- Do you work too much?
- Do you earn too little?
- Do you hate your job?
- Do you have problems with your relationships?

Right now, list the five things in your life you would most like to change for the better.

1. _____
2. _____
3. _____
4. _____
5. _____

Now list the five things you must *do* in order to implement these changes.

1. _____
2. _____
3. _____
4. _____
5. _____

Now list the five main reasons why you feel you cannot achieve these things or at least start in their pursuit today. For example, you feel you need more education, more money, or a better location.

1. _____
2. _____
3. _____
4. _____
5. _____

Now look carefully at the reasons you gave for why you can't make these changes now. Are they legitimate reasons for inaction or is there a hidden reason holding you back? Be very honest about the root cause of your inaction. Let's look at the situation another way.

How many of your reasons for inaction would still hold up if I told you that as a reward for achieving the first change on your list I would give you $1,000,000 in cash, tax-free. Would the prospect of such a handsome reward motivate you to achieve your first objective regardless of the negatives you feel are working against you? For instance, could such a grand reward motivate you to conquer your fear of looking stupid?

I'll put this example another way in case you are negatively motivated. What would happen if I told you that if you fail to achieve the first change on your list within twelve months from today you will be shot at dawn. Now don't just laugh; mentally put yourself in the position of being executed for your inaction. See yourself blindfolded and feel your back against a cold brick wall. What did you eat for your last meal? Can you still taste it? What was your last request? Hear the captain yell "Ready!" "Aim!" Now, do the reasons you wrote down for not achieving your objectives still hold up in the face of death? Could you conquer your fear of looking stupid if you knew that your life depended on it?

I'll bet in your case the answer to either scenario is yes. Yes you can break down the barriers that are holding you back. In the face either of a $1,000,000 reward or of death most of the reasons and fears for not achieving your objectives vanish.

> "I'd like to make more money but I'm not good at selling" is replaced by "Well, I could take some courses and become a better salesperson."
>
> "I want to move and get a better job but I must think of my mother" is replaced by "I could move to the nearest big city and get a better job or even start a business of my own. Then I could visit mother on weekends or even move her out here into a better neighborhood."

Whatever limitations are hindering you now, write them down. Confront them! Then cast them behind you forever. Develop an "I can do it" attitude and free yourself from limitations. There are multitudes of millionaires and you can be one simply by doing the same things they did. If you want to start a small business but lack the knowledge to run it—get it! If you don't have the qualifications to move up in your company, get them or get a new company!

Hundreds of thousands of people just like you have become millionaires in America. Some are young, some old, some highly educated, many others with no education at all. The one thing they all have in common is the ability to remove mental limitations that prevent them from living their dreams.

You are a manifestation of your own beliefs and attitudes. Your life and the success you achieve in it are governed only by your beliefs. You can achieve whatever it is you think you can achieve.

Reach for the Stars and You Just Might Hit the Ceiling

Think back for a while to the time when you where a child.
Go back to the time when you were six or seven years old.
Can you remember what you wanted to be when you grew
up? A cowboy like the ones in the movies? A princess? Or
was it a astronaut? Maybe it changed from day to day; it
didn't matter then. Whatever it was you wanted to do
when you were six or seven, the chances are very high
that's not what you are doing now with your life. Those
early ambitions gave way to new ones in your teens; then
eventually you settled for the compromise that is your
present job and lifestyle.

Can you remember what you dreamed of as a very
young child? Maybe it was cops and robbers battling it out
in the city. Perhaps it was princes and princesses romanc-
ing in stone towers, watching knights in armor battle evil
at the foot of the castle walls.

In your mind, can you still hear the sound of swords
clashing as your band of pirates captures a ship? Can you
hear the sound of exotic birds as you explore yet another
tropical island in search of hidden treasure? Can you remember the sight of 60,000 fans jumping to their feet as
you hit your dream grand slam in the bottom of the ninth
in the final game of the World Series? Your dreams were
limitless in their scope, imagination, and possibilities.

The chances are not only that you remember some of
these dreams but that you were also the key player in all
them. It wasn't your best friend who was prince or princess
while you were the court jester—it was you up there on the
throne with the golden crown. The fearless pirate leader
was not the boy or girl down the street; it was you, wasn't
it? It wasn't just any player hitting the final home run, it
was you. Nothing seemed impossible back then because
nothing was. It was in those wonderful years before the

negative conditioning you received on a daily basis began strangling your mind. Remember what they said?

"Are you day dreaming again? Hey you in the back! I'm talking to you!"

"Don't be a dreamer."

"It's a tough world out there. You have to be realistic."

"It's not easy to become successful."

"You have to work too hard to make any money."

It's too bad that at the time when these thoughts began registering in your mind you didn't know how important it was to limit their impact. When you were a child your mind was free of this negative conditioning, so, for example, you didn't instinctively hate people because of their color or creed. Nor did you think much about how you looked because you took the way you looked for granted. That was just how you were. It was not until people started telling you that you were pretty or ugly that you began to question yourself. Most experts agree that it is in these early years that the pattern of our lives is set.

Do you still dream big dreams? Do you dream of success and its rewards or are you too busy dealing with life? Do you think that your life will never be what you really want it to be? If so, it is time to remove these limitations from your mind and go back to being the child who knew that nothing is impossible.

As Napoleon Hill stated in his masterpiece, *Think and Grow Rich,* "What the mind can conceive and believe it can achieve." Or as Henry Ford said, "Whether you think you can or you think you can't—you are right."

On medieval maps all uncharted territory was marked with a picture of a dragon. This was a sign to sailors that they were entering unknown waters and should therefore proceed at their own risk. Some sailors took this sign literally and were deathly afraid to venture on for fear of the dragons they might encounter. Others saw killing dragons as an opportunity to become a hero or to discover great treasure. Such is life; it is full of dragons. You must decide here and now whether will you slay them or run from them. Start right now by slaying your own mental dragons and begin living your life to its true potential.

Resolve now to cast behind you all forms of mental limitations. Say out loud "From this point on I will not be held hostage to mental limitations. I can do whatever I choose to do and go as far as I want to go." As Franklin D. Roosevelt said "The only thing we have to fear is fear itself."

LESSON 2

HOW TO BE A
LUCK MAGNET

Luck is the residue of design
—BRANCH RICKEY

Y ou often hear people say that the way to get ahead in life is to know the right people. They say that making it big is just a matter of being in the right place at the right time and that you must be lucky in order to be promoted, to be noticed, and to become wealthy. In fact, most people feel that they actually have very little control over the events in their life, blaming their lack of success on some impersonal force in the great scheme of things that has somehow robbed them of the right to meet the type of people or discover the kind of opportunities that could contribute to their success. They feel that fate has dealt them a losing hand and that luck is simply not on their side.

Do you think this is true? Let me assure you it is not. While there are some things that are beyond your control, 99 percent of what is commonly called luck is actually subject to you. People can be a great help in reaching your goals and there are many ways you can bring these people into your life. Opportunities others typically regard as being the result of luck can be brought directly into your path through careful planning and action.

I am amazed at the number of people who think that they have bad luck or no luck at all. If luck were a fifty-fifty proposition with half of the population with it and half without, then the chance of you being lucky would be one in two. If this were indeed the case it would mean that there would be a lot more lucky people around. In reality, however, a full 75 percent of the population thinks that they are unlucky. They are wrong.

WHAT IS LUCK?

Luck, in short, is the crossroad where planning meets opportunity. If you miss an important job interview because your car develops a flat tire en route, is it the result of luck? Not if you were driving around on bald tires and without a spare for six weeks. Not if you didn't leave early enough to get a taxi or to hitch a ride in case of an emergency. Not if you had no money in your pocket to make a phone call or pay a cab. What could be called bad luck is really just a lack of planning and poor judgment.

If you have not developed a plan, set forth strategies, and taken positive action toward your goals (complete with back up ideas and strategies, which we will discuss later) you simply are not prepared to take advantage of an opportunity. Therefore you will not increase your chance of being "lucky" to any significant degree. If on the other hand you have done some or all of these things then your chances of being "lucky" are greatly enhanced. Let me give you some examples.

The Practice of Luck

When Gary Player, the South African golfer, first came to the United States in the late 1950s, he quickly began beating many of the local players. Soon, he had developed a reputation among them for being a lucky golfer. As most people do when faced with someone who is more successful, many of the regular tour pros simply decided that the reason Gary Player was winning was that he was luckier than they were.

When asked about this lucky reputation by a reporter, Player summed up his feelings in just one line, paraphrasing a quote from Thomas Jefferson: "Sure I'm lucky," he said, "and the more I practice the luckier I get."

Think carefully about those words because they hold the key to dramatically improving your luck: practice. The other pros of Player's day did not want to admit that he practiced harder than they did, hitting ten times more shots on the range, thus grooving and refining his swing. They didn't mention that he arrived before dawn and stayed until after dusk. That he went to bed early, avoiding parties and hangovers. Nor did they consider that he made up for his small stature by a rigorous program of exercise and muscle building long before it was fashionable. They simply dismissed his fine performance as being "lucky" because it was easier than facing the truth: He was better than most simply because he tried harder.

People are no different today than they were thirty or forty years ago. Ask a struggling musician how rock star Bruce Springsteen became so successful that he is now simply referred to in the music business as "The Boss." Most will dismiss any further discussion of the subject with a quick "Well, his music is good and he got lucky." The fact is he worked hard. Ask a novel writer trying to make it to the top of his craft how Stephen King became such a huge success. Again, the majority will quickly answer that he was simply lucky. Ask a corporate vice president why he was passed over for promotion and he will quickly rationalize that his competitor was lucky and had inside connections with the board. It never occurs to him to ask why his competitor had inside connections and he did not. It is simply easier to put it down to luck or a lack of it than to admit that laziness in developing contacts was the real reason the opportunity was lost.

Once you realize and accept that you make your own luck, you will improve your life quickly and easily and in many ways. Indeed, your eyes open to a host of new opportunities every day.

HOW TO GET LUCKY AND MEET ALL THE RIGHT PEOPLE

Do you think you are lucky? I don't mean just because you have your health and live in America (that of course automatically qualifies you as lucky) but I mean do you feel truly lucky? Do things seem to have a way of working out for you? Would you say that you are lucky only some of the time? Or do you feel you have very little luck at all?

Right now, on a scale of one to ten, with ten being very lucky, how would you rate your luck so far today? How about this week? The past month? The past year? What about your entire life up to this point?

If you came up with less than stunning answers to those questions, then it's time for you to take control of your luck. If your answers were good, then it's time to make them even better.

Remember what I said was the key to luck? *Practice.* It's true. Practice will make you a luckier person. As you apply the strategies and ideas in this lesson you will find that the people you need to help you will be brought into your life. New opportunities will suddenly appear. Soon, people will be telling you how lucky you are. Then you too can tell your friends and foes alike "The more I practice the luckier I get."

How to Not Attract Luck

Before I show you how to improve your luck, let me give you a typical example of how to not attract it. The passion of a young friend of mine is sailing and he is very good at it. When he came to California he wanted to find someone who was sailing a boat to the Bahamas, the Caribbean, or to Hawaii so he could join them and gain experience. He also wanted to see a nice part of the world. It was a very worthy and interesting goal and he had certainly chosen the right place to start.

Newport Beach and Dana Point harbors were just a thirty-minute drive from where he was staying. They are among the richest and most famous harbors in America. Long Beach harbor and Marina Del Rey were just another hour away. Each one of these fine harbors are full of giant yachts, ships, and boats of every kind, setting sail daily for all parts of the globe. Southern California is in fact the perfect place to find the ride of your dreams to any port in the world.

As a young single man he spent two or three nights a week at the local bars. However, instead of hanging out in the bars and clubs near the harbors where he would have mingled with other boaters, millionaires, and captains he chose to spend his time at a local hole-in-the-wall closer to his home. The bar was twenty miles inland and was frequented by a group of middle-aged bikers.

Although he made occasional day trips down to the harbors to inquire if anyone might be looking for help, he soon became discouraged. He could not find anyone to sail with and so he left California and returned home convinced that he had been "unlucky" and therefore did not find a boat on which to crew.

Be in the Right Place at the Right Time

Now that's a simple but very telling illustration. Virtually every week of your life you will run across someone with a similar hard-luck story. Most people don't realize that it is just not that hard to meet the right people if you actually set out each day trying to meet them!

Now in California every teenage boy knows that if you want to meet girls you go to the beach. No problem. But let's suppose you have a great script for a movie—where do you go? If you want to meet movie people, hang out in the Polo lounge at the Beverly Hills Hotel. Now that doesn't mean that by hanging out there for a week you are going to meet Steven Spielberg, but if you eat lunch there once a week, have a drink at the bar now and again, and make it one of your regular hang out, sooner or later you will meet someone who will look at your script or who knows someone who will.

If you are looking to move to another company in search of a better job, find out where the movers and shakers in your target company eat lunch or have cocktails. Make their place your place. Also find out where they go for recreation. Do they frequent a tennis club? The gym? Compete in a bowling league? Find out what they do and where they do it. How? Ask their friends, coworkers, secretaries— their competitors are great sources of information! Just find out something about the people you need to meet in order to improve your life. Read trade magazines and local papers to determine their interests. Play Sherlock Holmes. Investigate their hobbies, recreations, and hangouts. If all else fails ask them what their interests are. Most people will be only too happy to talk about themselves.

Once you have discovered the type of information you are looking for, take direct action so you will cross the path of those people you need to meet, in either a business or a social situation. Social situations are generally better since people tend to let down their guard when socializing.

Here is a simple and practical example of this type of luck in action. Recently, while chatting with a neighbor, I discovered that a certain influential person had moved into the community in which I live. Eager to meet him I began taking a daily walk with my dogs down the street on which he had bought a home. After walking my dogs down the same route for over four weeks, I eventually

bumped into him at the small lake that was the turn
around point of my walk. As "luck" would have it he too
had a dog and, like mine, it loved to swim in the lake. As
the dogs played in the water I got the chance to meet this
person and talk with him for twenty minutes. I can now
count this powerful person among my friends because of a
meeting that did not come about through chance.

Now, let's take a very specific look at how to meet certain types of people in the right type of situations.

Play Golf.   Let's suppose that you want to meet some
sports or movie stars, business leaders, or politicians in a
relaxed and comfortable atmosphere. Where would you
meet them? I mean people like Michael Jordan, Sean
Connery, and Bill Clinton, or any number of the wealthi-
est and most successful business people in the world.

The answer is on the golf course, or more specifically
playing golf in pro-am tournaments. If you play in these
events you will meet people just like those mentioned
above. What if you can't afford to play? Then volunteer to
help marshal or organize and you will still get your chance
to mingle with these people. The entire PGA Tour is run
around charity organizations who provide voluntary support for their events.

I happen to love golf; it is my main interest in life. I
attended college on a golf scholarship, live in a country
club community, and plan my schedule around the tournaments I want to watch or participate in. With the sole
exception of my good friend David Miller, every person I
have met who has helped me, provided counsel, or has
generally influenced my life in a meaningful way I met on
the golf course.

According to the National Golf Foundation, over
twenty-six million Americans play golf—that's ten percent
of the entire population. If you look at the number of powerful executives, business leaders, politicians, sports per-
sonalities, and movie stars who play golf you will find that

the percentage is actually much higher. In fact the number may well be as high as 30 or 40 percent. This means that two or three influential people out of every five you meet will play golf.

Now if there is one thing all golfers love regardless of their differences, it is talking golf. Golf seems to consume a person far more than any game known to man. Talk golf to golfers, or more specifically invite them to tell you about their game, and you will have developed the most sought after of all communication skills, instant rapport.

Golf is the ultimate game for meeting powerful and interesting people. You meet them away from the work environment, in a beautiful setting without any interruptions. You are with them for over four hours in the close confines of a golf cart, and between the actual shots you have a great deal of time to pick their brain or get your point across. No other sport offers the same opportunity for casual conversation, shop talk, and the development of friendships.

Mark McCormick, author of several books including *What They Don't Teach You at the Harvard Business School,* which I highly recommend, says "You can learn more about a person in one round of golf than in a hundred business meetings." I know from experience that this is true. People open up to you on a golf course. They tell you things about their wants, needs, desires, and problems. Armed with this type of information you can help these people further their goals while at the same time allowing them to help you reach yours.

If you do not play golf now and want to meet the right people, seriously consider learning the game. The better you play the more desirable you are to play with. Golfers as a whole enjoy playing with better players. They will look to you for club selection, for how to read the greens, and for other golf tips. This furthers your opportunity to develop a good relationship with them.

If you play but are a poor player take lessons from your local pro. You may also attend one of the many fine golf schools around the country, such as the Golf University in San Diego or Jimmy Ballard's Golf School at the Palm Beach Polo Club in Florida. They have a fabulous program for improving your game quickly, which is well worth the investment both in pleasure to you and for future business use.

If you do play now, make it a point to play in tournaments away from your own club where you have the opportunity to make new contacts, play in pro-ams whenever possible, and tee it up at your own club with different people on a regular basis. Golf clubs tend to be very cliquish. Once a group of people like each other they tend only to play with each other. That's fine up to a point but don't get caught in the trap of playing exclusively with the same people. Make an effort to show up occasionally at a different time just to meet some new faces. Every new face is a new person who may be someone you need to meet.

Playing in club tournaments will also give you the opportunity to mix with other players in the club. The more people you meet the more "luck" you will have in running into people who are ready and willing to help you or to refer you to others who can.

If You Don't Play Golf at Least *Talk* Golf.   If you don't play golf read golf books such as *Great Golf Stories* or *The World Atlas of Golf*. These will give you an overview of the major courses, players, and events. This alone will prove to be a great icebreaker with people who like to play golf. Just ask them to fill you in on your limited knowledge of the Masters tournament, for example, then sit back and listen. Golfers love to talk golf and if you can bring yourself to do nothing more than listen intently you will have developed a friend for life.

If you are young an alternative way to meet golfers is to work part-time at a golf club in the bar, cart barn, or bag room. There are many ways you can meet people around a golf course. When I was just 18 years old I met enough kind people while working in the bag room at the Wellington Country Club in West Palm Beach, Florida, that in just six months I was able to invite my two best friends over from England and travel with them up the eastern coast of the United States and into Canada. I was making just $3.50 an hour cleaning clubs and picking up range balls and yet the people I met helped me out immensely.

The three of us traveled from southern Florida through North Carolina to Virginia, then to Washington, D.C., New York City, Ottawa, and Toronto. Throughout our entire eight-week tour we played at the best country clubs, ate at the best restaurants, slept in the best parts of town, and saw all of the sights that part of the country has to offer. We spent just one night in a hotel and that only as a courtesy to our host because we drove into town late. The rest of the time these three 18-year-old kids with just a few dollars to their name stayed as the VIP guests of people I helped as a bag boy at the country club.

If golf is just not your thing and you can't bring yourself to show an interest in the game join a tennis club, Rotary club, Lions club, or some other type of organization that you know will bring you into weekly contact with the most influential and potentially helpful people in your community. The first rule of getting lucky is to develop a strategy to get out there and meet the type of people that can assist you in getting lucky.

Support Your Local Charity. Another great way to meet the people you want to meet is to involve yourself in charitable work. The great thing about doing charity work is that it pays off twice. First, it gives you the great feeling of have helped a good cause. Second, it can help you further your own goals.

I do not know of one famous or influential person who is not involved in doing some work for charity. Find out through newspapers or magazines or by asking directly which charities the person you want to meet is involved in. In the case of celebrities a call to their manager is the best and quickest source of information. For a corporate executive watch the newspapers and trade journals or ask his or her secretary.

Let's say it is essential to your overall plan that you meet the mayor of your city. Call up the mayor's office and find out what type of charities he or she is involved in. Once you know, call back a few weeks later with a plan to help raise funds for that charity: a car wash, a sponsored swim, or a walk with your little league team. Once you have developed your idea ask if the mayor would like to help out. Stress the potential public relations benefits and the media coverage of your event.

I have a good friend in New Jersey who used this very idea to get the mayor of his small town involved in his health club business. Soon the mayor was opening up all kinds of other doors for him. My friend became involved with the police and fire departments and with several local schools. This increased his recognition and his business in the community jumped dramatically in just six months. All this came about simply because he helped the mayor's favorite charity. And why not? That's what life is all about: You help my cause and I will be more than happy to do what I can for you.

A few years ago I wanted to get some press for a golf tournament I run in California. I called the editor of a local magazine and told him that I wanted to give some of the money I made to charity. Since I was new in the area and had not been involved with any specific charity, I asked whether he could suggest one that would be worthy of my support. Well, of course he could! Not only did he suggest one, but he suggested the charity of which he was chairman. Now he had a vested interest in supporting the event, so he also offered to publish a feature article on my golf tournament at no cost. This not only helped with the tournament but it also began a relationship that in turn helped several of my clients when they needed public relations help for their businesses.

It is not just the famous people who can help you further your goals. Often a stranger who may not be famous, powerful, or even particularly successful can clue you in to an opportunity.

Talk to People on Planes, on Trains, and in Lines. Actually talk to them. The average person knows approximately 250 people, successful people know four or five times that many. I travel a lot for a living, going from city to city speaking to groups at seminars and conventions. One thing that is truly amazing to me is how few people actually speak to each other. I see people sitting right next to each other on a plane for five solid hours who say nothing other than, "Excuse me. Can I get out please?" I ride trains, airport shuttles, and taxis and the people I see seldom speak. Instead, they sit in silence staring out the window. I'm sure you have noticed this yourself. If you want to get your life on the fast track you must make the effort to change this situation. Why? Because you never know who you might meet!

I always make it a point to start a conversation as soon as I come into direct contact with someone new. As they sit down next to me I ask, "What book is that you have? Is that author good?" I try to pick a question that engages the person in conversation. "What a nice watch you have. What make is it?" works well, as does, "What programs do you run on your laptop?" Ask any question that is likely to get the person speaking with you.

Whatever you use to break the ice (we will talk more about this in lesson seven), make it a habit to break it first. People often are shy or feel awkward talking to strangers, so help them out. Take the initiative by making the first move, then make them feel comfortable with you. You will be amazed by the many interesting and potentially useful people you will meet in the most unlikely places if you will only make the effort. Try to be outgoing; the worst that can happen is that someone may not want to talk. The chances are good, however, that they will talk and be glad that you made the effort to break the ice.

I recently came back from a weekend ski trip to Big Bear, California. During the short time I was there I met the drummer from a major rock group who lives on a farm and shares my wife's love of horses; an Englishman from Liverpool who imports handmade sports cars to America; the president of a large fund-raising company; and the owner of a wonderful local restaurant. I met each of them while taking the ten-minute ride to the top of the ski lift. I got the name and phone number of each and in time they may well help me or I them. I find meeting new and interesting people on the lift every bit as much fun as skiing down the mountain. All you have to do is talk!

How many new people have you met this month? Not many? Then you are either hanging out in the wrong places or wasting your chances through inaction.

List five people right now who have the knowledge, skill, or power to help you achieve your goals.

1. _____
2. _____
3. _____
4. _____
5. _____

Now list five ways in which you could meet these people. What charities do they support? Do they play golf? Do they frequent certain restaurants?

1. _____
2. _____
3. _____
4. _____
5. _____

SOME PEOPLE JUST DON'T GET IT!

A favorite television commercial of mine is one of the original ads for MTV. In the commercial a combat-clad Fidel Castro yells insults at the TV as it blasts out American rock music.

He yells, "Capitalist! Imperialist! American dogs!" and so on for about twenty seconds. Halfway through the spot, a British pop star comes on the screen and in his best cockney accent says, "MTV. Some people just don't get it!" And it's true: Some people just don't get it.

You're reading this book because you want to move up in the world, improve your life, and increase your self-fulfillment and finances. But many of those around you want you to keep on doing whatever it is you are doing now. They are happy with you just the way you are.

You see, the truth is that while there are many people out there that can help you move forward, there are a great many more who will try to hold you back or keep you in your comfort zone, either consciously or subconsciously. They don't understand that you are committed to living your life to your full potential.

Don't Waste Your Time with People Who Do Not Share Your Goals, Vision, or Dreams

As time goes by, people change. It is rare that your best friends in high school, in college, or at your first job will remain your close friends later in life. This is because unless they move forward at the same pace as you they get left behind. You could, of course, choose to remain stagnant and travel within a limited circle of friends with them, but you owe it to yourself and those who rely on you to move forward.

In order to make it big you must spend most or all of your time with people who are richer, smarter, or more successful than you. Unless your friends share your dreams they are destined to be left behind as you move up. There is nothing cold or callous about this; it's just a fact of life: some people grow and move toward their dreams and others stand still or shrink away from them.

If you continually play tennis with a friend that you can beat easily you will never improve your game. Your serve will not be tested, your backhand will remain so-so, and your forehand will never become really powerful. Why? Because you don't have to be better than you are now in order to win. You are never forced to improve your skills.

So it is in life. Although you may be the leader of your group of friends, you're just a big fish in a tiny pond. You must expand your friendships beyond your comfort zone in order to meet people whose wit, power, and success will challenge you.

Most unsuccessful people simply have no real desire to be successful. They will become envious when you start to move ahead. So don't be surprised when they try to bring you down. Often they themselves do not realize what they are doing; their methods are subtle. At other times they'll drop a few sarcastic comments here and there like, "I hope Frank still talks to us when he gets promoted" or "Remember us when you are a big star."

It is easy to spot this type of negative character if you open your ears. Unsuccessful people say things like:

- It can't be done.
- It won't work.
- Your idea is stupid.
- Don't work so hard. Just enjoy yourself.
- Don't move to another city or part of the country: you won't like it there.

In short, they'll do whatever they can to sabotage your success. If you do well, that makes them look bad. They would have to admit to themselves and others that you were somehow better and this is simply too much to ask of most people. Therefore, instead of allowing you to reach greatness they must try and drag you back down to their level. Do encourage your negative friends to pursue success and to join you on your journey, but if they refuse to follow your example slowly distance yourself from them. You have better things to do than waste your time on negative people.

How to Recognize Successful People

While unsuccessful people try to limit your dreams, successful people generally want you to share in their success and will encourage you to rise with them. Successful people say things like:

- Give it a shot!
- Go for it!
- Take a chance!
- What have you got to lose?

Successful people encourage you to pursue success by talking about its rewards. Learn to spot these people quickly; they are the type of people you are looking for as friends and associates.

To help create luck in your life, learn to identify lucky (better known as successful) individuals so that their "luck" can rub off on you.

In general, highly successful people get up early in the morning and go to bed early at night. This gets them to work hours before the rest of the world is even awake. It's like showing up to race before the other competitors have even arrived. Therefore early mornings and weekends are often the best times to catch up with them.

Successful people tend to dress well. This does not mean that they will always be found wearing a tuxedo or

European suits but they will dress for the occasion in quality clothing. Successful people walk with purpose and play with purpose. In fact, they do very little without a purpose. Learn to recognize their purpose so you can join them. Remember: Birds of a feather *do* flock together.

Every time you meet or engage in conversation with a successful person, you are increasing your chances of becoming lucky. Every time you go to a charity event, social function, or business club or just talk to the person next to you in line at the post office you are increasing your chances of meeting that special person willing to help you reach your goals. Meeting new people and talking with them is one of the key ways of discovering new opportunities. Starting now, make it a point to see how many new people you can meet. Challenge yourself to meet five interesting people this week. Set a goal for a specific number of people to meet this month or this year, then reward yourself when you reach your goal. Surround yourself with successful people.

CREATE LUCK IN YOUR PERSONAL LIFE

Americans spend over $200 million a year on amulets and good luck charms. While that's great for the economy, it makes you wonder what control people have over their destiny. The key to creating luck in your personal life is to take care of the little things over which you do have control. These are the mundane tasks that build up over time and contribute to your "bad luck" if not taken care of. (When they are taken care of the way they're supposed to be, no one ever mentions them as good luck. In fact, they're never mentioned at all.)

Have your car serviced regularly; go to the doctor and dentist for regular checkups. Don't drink and drive; do eat the right foods. Everything in moderation. Take home a gift for your spouse tonight; give an employee an extra day off. Go out of your way to find that book your boss has been looking for. Most of these things are just common sense. But that doesn't mean they are adhered to by many people. Planning, even at the simplest level, will improve your luck dramatically.

You may let all these simple little things slip your mind, but the next time you find yourself singing the blues over your hard luck, think again. Remember this advice and then consider how your present situation could have been avoided by previous action and simple planning. Take care of the little things in your life that often go wrong and you will soon find that the bigger things are starting to go right.

CREATE LUCK IN YOUR BUSINESS AND CAREER

One of the most prominent themes in the ads for state lotteries is "You can't win if you don't play." It's true. Opportunities for business and career advancement will not come if you do not take action to create them. It is a simple fact that the more resumes you distribute the more chance you have of getting an interview. The more sales calls you make the more chance you have of selling something. The more times you go to bat the more chance you have of hitting a home run.

The people who make the most effort to move forward in life are the people who are also labeled "lucky." The odds, of course, are simply on their side. Lucky people are not afraid of failure because they know that each time they fail the odds are irrevocably increased in their favor. Lucky people are persistent people and persistent people are lucky.

It's time for you to take charge and create some luck. Make plans now to be the luckiest person you know.

How many really interesting people have you met in the last six weeks?

What were their names?

1. _____
2. _____
3. _____
4. _____
5. _____

When do you plan to follow up by contacting these people?

Where do you go now that brings you into contact with other people who may help you? List five places such as church, bars, teams, social groups.

1. _____
2. _____
3. _____
4. _____
5. _____

Look at your list. Do these places bring you into contact with the right kind of people—positive, motivated, supportive, success-oriented people?

List five other places, associations, or groups in your area where you can contact others who may be able to offer you help or guidance.

1. _____
2. _____
3. _____
4. _____
5. _____

Resolve now to create luck in your life by being in the right places at the right times surrounded by the right people.

LESSON 3

USING GOALS TO
ROCKET YOU TO SUCCESS

I f you read the biographies of successful people you will
find that they all have something in common: They set
goals. Successful people start with a clear picture of
what they want to happen in their life, then they determine the steps they must take in order to realize their
dreams. If you want to move yourself into the five percent
of people who are at the top, you must learn to set goals
too.

Most Americans have only two goals: to pay the rent
and to keep their car from being repossessed. Sure, there
are many other things they would like to have like more
money and the respect of others, but few are prepared to
commit the time or effort (although it demands little of either) to write down their goals and draw out a road map
for their future.

The chances are that you have already heard or read
something about the value of setting written goals. Nevertheless, I'll bet that you do not have a clear, extensive set

of goals written down. In fact, studies show that less than five percent of the people in the country have taken the time to write out their goals in detail and to develop an action plan to realize them.

Why don't people draw up written goals? Some people do not write out their goals because they are afraid of failing to reach them. There is something about committing goals to paper that seems to carve them in stone. You can't wriggle out of something that is right there in black and white. If for any reason you do not accomplish a goal, you can't tell yourself that you didn't really want to or that you did not mean to—written proof is irrefutable.

A second reason that people do not commit their goals to paper is because they just don't have any goals or at least not any clear ones. Is this true of you? If so, then you must make a decision about what you really want from your life. What is it that you would do if money were no object? If you could spend your life doing whatever you like to do, what would it be? Would you travel the world? Would you spend your days fishing? If the genie from Aladdin's lamp suddenly appeared and gave you three wishes how would you use them to change your life?

Let me suggest another method to help you discover goals. Ask yourself the following questions: What would you do in the next twelve months if you knew it was to be the last year of your life? What would you want to see, do, and achieve in that time? The answers to these questions will help you come up with a list of activities that can be turned into goals.

The final reason that many people do not set written goals is that no one has clearly described to them the importance of doing it. Take it from me, if you do not take the ten to fifteen minutes it takes to fill out the goals section of this book, you will have little chance of getting where you want to go. How can you, if you don't know where you are going? You can't.

Quick! Get in your car and drive to Transylvania, Arkansas. Don't look at a map! Don't ask anyone for directions! Just drive! What are your chances of finding Transylvania, Arkansas? Pretty small without getting hopelessly lost. I know, I was hopelessly lost when I found it! But seriously, written goals are like a good road map.

HUNTING FOR TREASURE

Let's say you enter a treasure hunt that has a $1 million cash prize for the winner. Their are nine other people in the contest. The treasure is buried somewhere in Yellowstone National Park and nine of you are given certain vague clues as to where it is located.

You are told that it can be found within sight of the tallest peak, it is close to an area popular with bears, and that it is off the main roads. All these clues lead you to within a twenty-mile radius of the treasure. It's not much to go on, but it's a start.

The tenth person, however, is given a map. The map does not have all of the road names, rivers, or significant trees on it, but it does have the major landmarks and a clear indication of where the treasure is buried.

You are all dropped off in different locations on the perimeter of the park. Who do you think is going to find the treasure first? Obviously, the person with the map. Let me ask you another question: Do you feel that the person with the map has an unfair advantage?

Most people would say "Yes!" and yet it is exactly the type of advantage that is enjoyed by people who have drawn up written goals and action plans. It is also the type of advantage that you will enjoy when you have completed this lesson. The simple act of writing down your goals will vault you into the 5 percent of people in the country who have done so. It will also dramatically increase your chances of making it big.

MY LESSON

I consider myself very lucky in that ever since I was seven years old I have had very clear goals. I have always known what I wanted from my life. Although I have found it necessary to adjust my goals from time to time, I have never lost sight of them.

One of my early goals was to have a large house with unique modern architecture. A house with high ceilings and an open floor plan. This house would also have lots of glass, a huge bathroom with a hot tub, and large, open spaces ideal for entertaining my friends. At the age of twenty-six I bought my first house and for a little over four hundred thousand dollars I got just what I wanted.

When I was about ten years old a man in our neighborhood bought a new Porsche Carrera. It was jet black with the Carrera letters running up the side in large gold script. It was then that I decided I had to have a Porsche.

When I was fifteen years old and almost old enough to drive, a friend's father gave me a ride home in his brand-new Porsche 928S. Immediately, I knew that this was the Porsche I wanted. It was the fastest, smoothest ride I had ever experienced. That night I made it my goal to have one.

Now, I did not know at the time how I was going to achieve this goal but I knew it would happen. To start things in the right direction I put Porsche pictures on my wall. I read all the literature on the 928 I could find, discovering how fast they were, where they were made, and so on. And at the age of twenty-seven I finally bought one. I even paid cash! Goals work.

The bottom line is this: the clearer your goals are to you, the easier it is for you to reach them. I used this principle during my first year in my karate studio. I decided I wanted to make one hundred thousand dollars. I had never made that much money in my life. In fact, I had never made more than fifteen thousand dollars in a single year, so it seemed like a lofty goal. Not only did I achieve this goal, but I even exceeded it. This verified my belief in goals, and they can work the same magic in your life. In order to help you make your goals work too, let's examine the process of goal setting.

SETTING GOALS

Imagine yourself on a sailboat without a rudder, floating around on the sea awaiting the wind to blow you into port. It's far more likely that you'll be wrecked on the rocks, isn't it? It's the same if you attempt to live without goals.

By defining goals, you add a rudder to your ship. Then you can trim your sails and head for the port of your dreams. You'll find opportunities appearing on your horizon and people entering your life to help make your goals happen. Your life will begin to change for the better. Talk to anyone who has set goals and they will tell you amazing stories of how things began coming together for them.

Goals focus not only the conscious mind but also the subconscious mind on a specific target. Once your mind is focused on a target it will do everything in its power to help you reach it. This is partly because your mind now knows exactly what you want, so it becomes sensitive to people and opportunities that will help you. Have you ever bought a car in an unusual color thinking it was unique, only to find that every other car on the road was the same color? The only thing that changed was that your brain became aware of that color and noticed it more often. It is the same with goals: Once you set them your mind will become sensitive to opportunities and ways in which the goals can be accomplished. Goals ultimately become the road map of your destiny giving your mind a clear and focused path.

Goals Must Be Specific

To make goal setting work well, you must make your goals specific. If you want to buy a house this year, don't just say, "My goal is to have a house this year." Find the one you want; walk through it. Help your mind focus on this particular house by putting a picture of it on your refrigerator. Know exactly how many rooms your new house has, the number of windows, what color it is, and what it smells like. Focusing on goals in this way makes your subconscious mind concentrate on reaching the goal. Besides zeroing in on the goal, you are also focusing on the feelings you're going to experience and on the importance of attaining this goal.

The human brain is an incredibly powerful, amazing piece of equipment. Yet we use only a fraction of its vast resources. The brain will do whatever you command it. If you tell it that your goal is to have a new four-bedroom house in a nice part of town, it will do everything in its power to help you get that house. If, however, you send a message to your brain that you would like the house, but also tell it all the reasons why you can't possibly have it, your brain will comply, working overtime to provide you with all kinds of reasons why you can't get the house. Your brain does whatever you tell it to do. Tell it to help you find ways to the top and that's exactly what it will do. Tell it to provide excuses to sabotage your success and it will do a stunning job. Be very, very specific when defining your goals.

Describe in detail your new house and how having it will make you feel. Will it be in a new upscale neighborhood with a country club? Will it be large and spacious with vaulted ceilings and lots of light or old with stained glass windows to show off all your antiques? The more detailed and specific you make your goals, the more you will do in order to achieve them. Make them real and you will be surprised just how quickly they happen.

Goals Must Be Compatible

The second thing you must consider when setting goals is to make sure they are in agreement with your other goals, beliefs, and values. Goals must be congruent with your true beliefs in order to thrust you forward. You will not reach your goal of making $1 million in sales this year if the computer equipment you are selling constantly breaks down and you know it's worthless. If you have any type of integrity at all, your subconscious mind will prevent you from reaching your goal.

At a recent seminar in Canada a young man told me that within five years he wanted a Ferrari Testarossa, a three-bedroom house on a nearby lake, and a boat. Now the young man had a growing business and was full of energy, enthusiasm, and the will to work hard. I didn't doubt that although his goals were lofty they were well within the bounds of possibility. However, he also stated that he would settle with making fifty thousand dollars a year. This is a perfect example of incongruent goals. You can't buy a two hundred thousand dollar sports car, a three hundred thousand dollar home, and a thirty thousand dollar boat if you only make fifty grand a year.

Had he moved forward without correcting this mindset, he would not have reached his goals because he was still confused about what he wanted. We went back through his goals together and reevaluated them so that they were in agreement with each other.

Here's a common example of incongruent behavior sabotaging success. Have you ever justified staying at a job you hated just so you could save enough money to bail out and do something you truly liked? It seldom works. You would have had a better chance of attaining your goals if you stopped doing what you hated and instead channeled your energy into doing something that you enjoyed.

I lived this myself, tired and bored with a business I founded. I drifted aimlessly for twelve months trying to justify selling it. I had no idea how I would replace the substantial income it provided, but I sold it anyway and jumped off the deep end hoping I could swim. Not only did I swim but I also began to have more fun than ever! It was as if a giant weight were lifted from my shoulders. I instantly became more creative and began to follow other opportunities that were of far more interest to me than my previous business. When you do what you truly love, something magical happens with your creativity and energy.

Goals Must Be Measurable

You must set goals that are measurable. Saying that you want to be comfortable, happy, or well off is not a goal that can be measured. You must set goals that allow you to check your progress toward them. Intangible goals cannot be measured, so they remain distant and unobtainable. Therefore, you'll want to set up a scale so you can track your progress by time, income, weight loss, or some other appropriate unit of measure.

Goals Must Be Achievable

In order to be reached, goals must be achievable. Now this allows for a great variety of goals because almost anything is achievable if you work hard enough. At this point it's not important how you are going to buy a boat and sail it around the world—somehow, someway that goal can be realized. It doesn't matter at this point that you have no money or sailing experience. It doesn't even matter that given your present circumstances the goal may seem impossible. Successful people routinely accomplish the impossible. The goal, however, must be achievable. In case it sounds like I am contradicting myself, let me you give two examples. One is of a seemingly impossible goal that can be accomplished, the other of a goal that is not achievable.

I know of a man who since he was a little kid wanted to go into space. When he first set this goal, John Glenn had not yet orbited the Earth. Today, this man is a multimillionaire and stays in great physical shape because there is talk of taking passengers up in the space shuttle. Despite the fact that people thought he was crazy when he first set his goal, he may yet achieve it.

On the other hand, there are unattainable goals, like that of the fifty-seven-year-old truck driver who wants to play starting quarterback for the San Francisco 49ers for a season. That is not a legitimate goal—it's a daydream that he cannot ever hope to achieve.

Goals can encompass almost anything you wish. Dream big! But do not confuse goals that only seem impossible with those that truly are. Seemingly impossible goals can almost always be achieved.

It is also important to set goals that you can directly control. Let me explain: Setting a goal to end world hunger is admirable. However admirable it is, though, it is not an attainable goal in that you cannot bring it about on your own. Setting a goal to marry a specific person is another example of a goal you cannot achieve without the help and consent of another person. You must have direct control over your goals.

Goals Must Be Personal

Your goals must be *your* goals—not the goals of your parents, spouse, or friends. You must want your goals and believe in them 100 percent or it is a waste of your time to

set them. Goals that others push on you will not be goals
that your mind will strive to achieve.

SETTING LONG-TERM GOALS

If you want to positively influence the course of your life
you'll need to set long-term goals. Set them and you will see
your life starting to change for the better. It's fun to watch.

In order to plan effective goals you must set them in
stages. First, you will set long-term goals of five, ten, or
twenty years. We'll call them "dream goals." These are the
things that you ultimately hope to do in your life. Then
you will back up and set interim goals to be reached in one
to five years. These we'll call "vision goals." Finally, you
will develop short-term goals of a year, a month, a week,
and even of a day. If you follow this method you'll start
with your ultimate goal and then work backward to see
what steps you must take in order to reach that pinnacle.

Start the goal setting process right now by taking out
a piece of paper and writing down 100 things that you
want to do, own, or accomplish in the next five to ten
years. Put no limits on their price or what you presently
think your chances of achieving them are. Call it a wish
list, a dream list, or a wants list—it doesn't matter. Just
pick up a pen and write. Do not stop to think; let the right
side of your brain take over. Throw logic out the window
for the moment. Don't put down your pen until you have
written all 100 things down.

To make this easy I am going to suggest a few categories for you to consider. You can always go back later and
add or delete them. First, list ten places in the world you
would like to visit over the next five years. Remember,
there are no limitations! So why not ski the Alps, snorkel
in Tahiti, and dine in Paris? Write down ten countries,
cities, or places that you have always wanted to visit.

1. _____
2. _____
3. _____
4. _____
5. _____
6. _____
7. _____
8. _____
9. _____
10. _____

Okay. You now have two great vacations a year to look forward to for the next five years. Now let's look at things a little closer to home. What kind of house do you want to own within the next five to ten years? List ten features of your dream home. Where is it? How big is it? How much land is it on? Does it have a garden? Do you have an office in it? Describe the pool area. Tell me right now what wonderful features your dream home contains. If you currently own your dream home, describe below the kind of second home or vacation home you would like.

1. _____
2. _____
3. _____
4. _____
5. _____
6. _____
7. _____
8. _____
9. _____
10. _____

Now list twenty material things that you want like a new car, boat, country club membership, entertainment system, pool table,—whatever! Remember to be specific: If you want a car specify the make, model, and color.

1. _____
2. _____
3. _____
4. _____
5. _____
6. _____
7. _____
8. _____
9. _____
10. _____
11. _____
12. _____
13. _____
14. _____
15. _____
16. _____
17. _____
18. _____
19. _____
20. _____

Now write down twenty ways you want to improve your personal life. How much money do you want to make? How much more time would you like to devote to work, golf, and your family. How would you like to improve your relationships? Where will your children go to college? Would you like to lose weight or increase your fitness level? These improvements don't have to be grandiose ideas; these goals can be as simple as allowing yourself time each day to take your dogs for a long walk. Write them down now.

1. _____
2. _____
3. _____
4. _____
5. _____
6. _____
7. _____
8. _____
9. _____
10. _____
11. _____
12. _____
13. _____
14. _____
15. _____
16. _____
17. _____
18. _____
19. _____
20. _____

Now write down twenty other goals that do not fit into any of the categories above. For example, how you might help others.

1. _____
2. _____
3. _____
4. _____

 5. _____
 6. _____
 7. _____
 8. _____
 9. _____
10. _____
11. _____
12. _____
13. _____
14. _____
15. _____
16. _____
17. _____
18. _____
19. _____
20. _____

Now go back through your list of one hundred items and number the ten most important goals right now, with number one being the most important of the ten and number ten the least important. These ten goals should be those accomplishments that would fulfill your ambitions and provide you with a real sense of achievement. Now write them down below.

My Top Ten Long-Range Goals Are

1. _____
2. _____
3. _____
4. _____
5. _____

6. _____
7. _____
8. _____
9. _____
10. _____

1. I will achieve goal one by_____.
2. I will achieve goal two by_____.
3. I will achieve goal three by_____.
4. I will achieve goal four by_____.
5. I will achieve goal five by_____.
6. I will achieve goal six by_____.
7. I will achieve goal seven by_____.
8. I will achieve goal eight by_____.
9. I will achieve goal nine by_____.
10. I will achieve goal ten by_____.

SETTING SHORT-TERM GOALS

Sometimes long-term goals appear so far away or over-whelming that they seem unreachable. That is why they must be broken down into short-term goals. Doing this will make the long-term goals more manageable and help you reach them faster.

For example, pretend your goal is to write a book. If you try to write a three hundred page manuscript in one sitting at your computer it won't happen. Even if you manage to write ten or twenty pages, page three hundred will still seem a world away.

A better way to approach this goal is to divide the book into four or five main sections. These sections in turn can be broken down into several chapters. Then break the chapters into a specific number of pages. Now when you sit in front of the blank screen you can think in terms of completing a chapter or even seven pages instead of facing the daunting task of finishing the whole book. Your mind will not wander to page three hundred and worry about what you must write there. Instead, you can focus solely on the seven to ten pages that you will write today. Tomorrow when you write another eight pages or so you will have completed an entire chapter. It is amazing how much more quickly you will achieve any task when you approach it this way.

Short-term goals encourage you to set priorities that will help you reach your long-term goals quickly. For example, if you are in sales and if your long-term goal is to make one hundred thousand dollars a year, your short-term goal could be to make two extra sales this week. If your long-term goal is to receive a promotion in your present company, your short-term goal could be to attend a seminar or course related to your business in order to increase your value to the company. If one of your long-term goals is to travel around the world, your short-term goal could be to see Mexico and Canada this year. By starting close to home you can quickly and inexpensively start off toward your ultimate goal.

Each short-term goal that is reached is another step up the ladder that leads to your ultimate goal. Although your dream goals may still seem a long way off you will quickly find that every step you take up the ladder allows you to see your destination more clearly. And the more clearly you can see your goals, the closer they will seem.

Short-term goals should be broken down into daily goals to help you keep on track. Here is an exercise to help you to prioritize your goals. Take a piece of paper and write down a goal for today. This goal can be very broad and could be something along the lines of finishing reading this month's trade journal, calling three former customers and getting at least one to come back, organizing your filing system, or investigating time management software for your computer.

Whatever your daily goals are, make them specific and reachable. Setting daily goals that cannot be realistically achieved for two or three weeks will not help you. Nor will making goals that are too easy to reach. Instead choose a number of simple but challenging goals each day that help you attain your ultimate goal.

While you are doing this, look for those activities that do not propel you forward and eliminate them. For example, when you are at work don't waste time reading the sports page. Instead, save that for when you get home. Scan the business page for any information that may be helpful in your job. Spend your lunch hour improving your skills by reading a book or listening to tapes as you eat, or eat with a prospective customer or an associate. Kill two birds with one stone!

Reward Yourself for Reaching Short-Term Goals

One way to make these short-term goals become a reality is to reward yourself for reaching them. It could be something as simple as drinking a cold beer after cutting the grass. Or get a little extravagant after achieving a particularly challenging goal: Buy yourself a new CD player for your car after slaving away all week to create an increase in business.

Strike a bargain with yourself: As you write down specific short-term goals include at the end of each set a small reward that will become due and payable to you on completion of these goals. The more challenging the completed goal, the larger the reward.

Do you understand the importance of rewarding yourself for reaching your goals? It focuses your mind on the

pleasant outcome reaching your goal will bring you instead of on the hard work that is necessary to get there.
Start thinking about the things you will enjoy in Palm
Springs. Once you get yourself in this frame of mind, picking up the phone to call a few extra customers will be
easier to do.

I mentioned my karate school earlier. Karate programs are designed with a reward system based on different colored belts. Let me tell you how incredibly effective
this is. When I first opened my karate studio, I was dis-
tressed by the number of people who quit after just three
months. I quickly realized that this was because for small
children (who constituted over 50 percent of my business)
waiting three months to be rewarded with a different colored belt was virtually equivalent to waiting half their life.

We changed our system so that at the end of four
weeks they tested for their first colored belt. This improved student retention immediately. By the time they
reached their third month they were preparing to test for
their third belt. Instead of being rewarded just once in
three months they were now rewarded three times in
three months. This kept the students interested and motivated, and it brought the school substantially more income
in the form of both monthly dues and testing fees. An additional benefit came from students proudly showing off
their new belts to friends and relatives, which in turn
brought in a great deal more referral business.

We increased motivation and retention even further
when we introduced a black uniform to replace the traditional white uniform as a special symbol of respect for those
who were members of the studio for six months or more.
With the prospect of such a reward, no one wanted to quit
before reaching the six month point, which had proven to be
another sticking point in student motivation. The point is
that rewarding yourself or others for reaching simple short-
term goals works. Set up a little reward system for yourself
today and it will help you move forward tomorrow.

PERIODICALLY REEVALUATE YOUR GOALS

Reevaluate your goals periodically and update or adjust them. The world and your life are in a state of constant change and movement. As you move forward toward your goals things will happen that may necessitate changing or modifying them. Some of these things will make reaching your goals easier, others will make it harder. The key is to be flexible enough to reevaluate and reprioritize your goals on a regular basis. For instance, if you develop a heart condition, the fitness and weight loss program that was fifth on your goal list should now move up in priority to first. This does not mean that you would ignore the other goals, just that your new goal of better health would take priority over all the others. In the absence of any major development, goals should be completely reviewed at least three or four times a year.

ALWAYS KEEP YOUR GOALS IN FRONT OF YOU

Use a daily planner to keep your goals in front of you on a daily basis. Use your planner to record your goals for the week. Put pressure on yourself to perform; don't leave the office until you have done everything in your power to make these goals happen.

The clearer you make your goals and the more often you write them down and reaffirm them to yourself, the harder your conscious and subconscious mind will work to help you achieve them.

One way to reinforce your goals is to create a color picture of you reaching them. If you are visually oriented and can do this in your head, fine. But if you are not visually oriented try making a picture of yourself surrounded by the things you want out of life. For example, if your goal is recognition and respect take a picture of yourself in a nice suit, then take some scissors and cut it out. Now paste your picture in the middle of another, perhaps of a stadium where everyone is cheering wildly, such as at a political convention. Now make color copies of your composite picture and place it on your refrigerator, on your closet door, on your desk, in your garage, and anywhere you will continually see it.

CREATE A SCRAPBOOK OF DREAMS

Another way to keep your goals constantly in mind is to make a scrapbook of your dreams. Every time you are looking through a magazine and see a car you would love to own, a place you would love to see, or a restaurant you would love to dine in tear it out and place it in your scrapbook. Refer to this book every week—better yet, look at it every night before you go to bed and every morning when you get up. The more often you clearly see the things you are working hard to achieve, the faster you will achieve them. Not only will your scrapbook stimulate your subconscious mind but it will also increase your motivation to succeed.

Resolve now to set the long- and short-term goals necessary to reach your ultimate goal. It will take discipline to do this, but it is crucial to success. If you follow the goal setting steps I have described, you can't help but be successful.

LESSON 4

PLANNING FOR SUCCESS

To fail to plan is to plan to fail
—BEN FRANKLIN

S am Walton, founder of the WalMart stores, often read in the newspapers about the overnight success of his stores and of his instant billionaire status. Sam's reply to these stories? "My overnight success, like most overnight successes, was twenty years in the making."

Lee Iacocca, one of the best-known managers in the world, responded in much the same way after being elected president of Ford Motor Company at age thirty-six. He said, "Suddenly after ten years of hard work I was an overnight success." Success is not an accident. Careful planning and thought are necessary to develop a winning strategy that enables you to reach your goals.

THE CAUSE OF ALL YOUR PROBLEMS

I have a little joke with my friends about the two simple causes of all problems: lack of talent or poor planning.

61

When you think about it, it is true, isn't it? I quote these reasons to my friends when they hit a bad golf shot and ask me what happened. I quote them to my staff when something goes wrong at the office and they turn to me for answers. I quote them to the people in my lectures and seminars. Next time something goes wrong in your life, look at these two simple reasons; you will see that at least one applies to your situation.

Lack of talent can be corrected by education and practice. We will discuss this later. Poor planning can often be solved with a blank sheet of paper and a pen. Writing things down is the best way ever devised to remember things, save time, forecast events, and plan for the future. Remember the words of Ben Franklin quoted above? Well they're true. Failure takes no planning or thought; it is easy to fail. Success takes planning and lots of it. The more detailed your action plan is the more quickly you will reach your goals. We will look at both macro and micro planning in this section, but first let's take a moment to figure out just where you are now.

WHERE ARE YOU NOW?

By now you have a series of written long- and short-term goals. But goals alone will not help you if you do not develop a detailed plan of action to reach them. Our action plan is composed of three parts: strategy, tactics, and logistics. Before we examine them further, let's take stock of where you are now. In order to do this you must analyze your SWOT, otherwise known as your Strengths, Weaknesses, Opportunities, and Threats.

Understanding your SWOT will give you a base from which you can attack your goals. In order to understand this, let's pretend that your ultimate goal is to climb Mount Everest. To make it to the very top in record time, you have assembled an experienced team of climbers and are now planning your strategy.

You have come up with the following basic SWOT:

Strengths

Having climbed all the other mountains in the Himalayas, you have a great deal of experience and practical knowledge. You also have a good, strong support team. Finally, you have plenty of corporate sponsors to fund the expedition.

Weaknesses

Your team is still a little tired from your last climb. Your best climber had to return home because his father is ill. He is unlikely to return in time for the expedition.

Opportunities

Your timing is great because it is the fiftieth anniversary of Hillary's conquest of Everest. A major network is going to sponsor and film the climb. The weather forecast is promising.

Threats

The government of the area is unstable and often creates last minute problems. A team of Japanese climbers is set to make a similar attempt two weeks later. Will your record time be fast enough to withstand their challenge? Going up in record time will mean taking less equipment, which will increase the danger.

Now that you see how a SWOT works, let's analyze your own situation.

What are your unique strengths? Are you a good salesperson? A good leader? Do you work with your hands well? What is it that you do best?

1. _____
2. _____
3. _____
4. _____
5. _____

What are your weaknesses? Are you disorganized? A procrastinator? What areas do you need to improve?

1. _____
2. _____
3. _____
4. _____
5. _____

What are your opportunities? Are there promotions in the wind? New markets to conquer? New businesses that are needed? What opportunities do you have?

1. _____
2. _____
3. _____
4. _____
5. _____

What are your threats? Are there others with a good chance at this promotion? Heavy competition for the new business you have planned? What are the potential problems?

1. _____
2. _____
3. _____
4. _____
5. _____

Once you have analyzed your SWOT you are ready to plan your strategy for reaching your goals. Taking into account the results of your SWOT you can plan your strategies around your weaknesses and play only to your strengths or you can take direct action to shore up your weaknesses. If, for example, you need better sales skills in order to achieve your goals for business growth you can seek better training for yourself or you can hire the services of a skilled salesperson—either solution shores up a key weakness.

ACTION STRATEGY

Once you have discovered exactly where you are now you are ready to begin your action strategy. These are the actions, tasks, and jobs that you must accomplish in order to reach your goals. Let's look at the actions you must take in order to reach your goal of climbing Everest.

1. You must secure permission from the Tibetan government as well as obtain entry visas and travel documents.
2. You must obtain $2 million to fund the climb.
3. You must coordinate your team of climbers.
4. You must gather together all the tents, rope, and climbing equipment that you need.
5. You must book the air and ground transportation to get you to Katmandu.

6. You must hire a team of Sherpa guides to help you up the mountain.

7. You must obtain sufficient stores of food and medical supplies to last the entire expedition.

8. You must persuade previous expeditions to lend you their maps, charts, and notes.

Now go back to Lesson Three to your list of top ten long-range goals and pick one. Write it down below. Under it list ten actions that you will need to take from start to finish in order to achieve this goal.

In Order to _____
I Must Take the Following Actions

1. _____
2. _____
3. _____
4. _____
5. _____
6. _____
7. _____
8. _____
9. _____
10. _____

Limiting Factors

Once your actions have been written out in black and white you must then decide which one of them is the limiting factor. Which is the action or skill that is needed in order to allow the other things to fall into place? You must identify this limiting factor and act on it first so as not to halt your progress. Very often people rush into projects without identifying the limiting factor. They spend their hard work on parts of the project that are eventually held up by other factors that should have been tackled first. This leads to frustration and often to failure. This can be avoided by tackling the limiting factor first.

For example, if you are an immigrant to America from a country in which English was not spoken and you want to make it big, your limiting factor is often your inability to speak English. You can only go so far without a command of the language. Everything else you do should take second place to learning English as quickly and as thoroughly as possible.

If you want to start you own business your limiting factor is often your ability to attract customers and get them to buy your product or service. If you lack marketing savvy and sales skills all your other knowledge and skills will be wasted until you learn or improve in these crucial and limiting areas. Or perhaps your limiting factor is a lack of cash, too many government regulations, or the 101 other things that crop up. Whatever your limiting factor is, act on it first and you will smooth the way ahead and make true progress toward your goals.

In the case of your Everest expedition, the limiting factor is obtaining permission from the Tibetan government to enter their country. Do you see how this is the key limiting factor? Without addressing this issue first all your other efforts will be wasted should the government deny your permit. What good is spending months gathering the needed equipment and funds only to find that you can't even set foot in the country?

Look at your list of ten actions you'll need to take in order to reach one of your top ten goals. Write down the chief limiting factor that must be overcome before any other steps are taken.

The Chief Limiting Factor Is

1. _____

Once the first limiting factor has been identified, go back through your list and prioritize the other items. What is the second most important factor? What is the third? In this way you will build a clear picture in your mind of what actions must be taken and in what order to reach your goals. Remember, the clearer you can picture your goals the faster you will be able to attain them.

TACTICS

Once all your actions have been listed you must turn to the actual tactics that you will employ to make your action plan a reality. Specifically, how will you handle each of these actions in order to ensure they are carried out correctly?

Let's go back to our example of climbing Mount Everest. The key limiting step is getting permission from the Tibetan government. What is necessary to overcome this obstacle? Let's break it down into specific tactics.

Who will get permission?

When?

How long will it take?

How much will it cost?

Where do you get such permission?

You have decided that this important step will be handled by you personally. So you call Washington to find out the answers to these questions. You find that it takes three months, costs two thousand dollars, and can be done through the Chinese embassy in Washington. You would then outline a substrategy for bringing this task to completion.

Now transfer what you've just learned to your own situation. Take the first action step you've written above. Underneath it write the specific tactics that you must use to make it happen, who will do it, when, and how?

The action step is_____.

The Tactics I Will Use to Accomplish This Step Are:

1. _____
2. _____
3. _____
4. _____
5. _____
6. _____
7. _____
8. _____
9. _____
10. _____

LOGISTICS

The third and final part of setting your action strategy is logistics. Do you have enough money, people, and equipment to make it to your goal? If not, to ensure your success, they must either be found before you start or be picked up along the way.

Now list the specific resources you will need to reach your goals. Whose help do you need? Where will the money come from? Will you need to hire new staff? Write your needs below.

In Order to Implement My Action Strategy
I Must First Secure the Following:

1. _____
2. _____
3. _____
4. _____
5. _____
6. _____
7. _____
8. _____
9. _____
10. _____

Set aside a weekend afternoon in a place where you will not be disturbed. If you must, get out of town! Go through the entire process listed above with each of the top ten long-range goals you listed in Lesson Three. Yes, I know it is work, but if you will do this you'll soon find yourself among the small percentage of successful people.

By now you have developed lists of written goals, of actions you must take in order to achieve your goal, of your chief limiting factor, of your first action step, of your tactics to accomplish this first step, and of your resources. If you have not yet completed this plan then go back and complete it now! I simply cannot stress too highly the value of writing things down in this manner.

MAKING TIME FOR SUCCESS

The biggest objection I hear from people attending my seminars is "Who has time for all this planning?" Well, what I've done above is establish the macro issues of planning for success. Now let's examine the micro issues of planning; how to use your time on a weekly, daily, and hourly basis most effectively to provide you with the time you'll need to plan your goals.

Your Time

One of the key problems you must solve on your road to success is planning and managing your time so you can reach your goals. At a recent seminar an attorney told me that he simply did not have time to plan changes in his life. This despite the fact that he was obviously far more interested in doing something else than in being an attorney. Yet if he can't find 10 or 15 minutes a day to plan, he can't expect to be successful.

In today's frenetic world the only way to create more time is to be ruthless in spending the little time you have. Successful corporations operate on this principle, beginning every new year with a detailed plan of how it will be run. Yet while the people working for these corporations take great care in planning at work, very few develop a personal plan of action.

There are twenty-four hours in a day, of which, if you're an average person, you spend eight hours at work and eight asleep. That leaves eight hours a day in which to do pretty much as you please. That works out to forty hours per week of free time during the work week, plus an additional thirty-two hours awake on the weekend. Even allowing for commute time and time spent eating, you still have a large amount of free time every week. The question is, how do you spend this time? Do you use it to further your goals or do you squander it watching soap operas or sports on TV every night? According to the Nielson company the average American watches seven hours of television a day! Contrast this with a Gallup poll revealing that over 50 percent of highly successful people watch less than an hour of television per day, with approximately 20 percent of that group watching none at all.

You spend, on average, twice as much time away from work than at it. So what should you do with all that free time? First, recognize that most successful people do not work only forty hours a week. They work fifty, sixty, or seventy hours a week. So start by applying at least eight of your free hours to your work or to the furthering of your career. If you have your own business it will be easy to spend an extra eight hours of work productively. If you work for someone else and the office is not open extra hours, take work home with you. Show your boss that you put in the extra effort that others do not.

Better still, you may want to use your extra time to start a business of your own. Something that fits in with your hobbies and can be fun as well as profitable, like selling baseball cards, stamps, or model planes. You could start up a mail order business, or maybe moonlight as a consultant selling your knowledge. Imagine the possibilities! If you invest your extra time developing these possibilities, you might just find that you can create a new career for yourself! This is just how many successful companies began.

Spend at least one hour a day on furthering your knowledge of your business or industry. Read trade journals; attend seminars; enroll in night school. This will take another seven hours from your free time, but you still have over fifty-seven left! You'll need a minimum of ten to fifteen minutes per day to plan for the next day. Reviewing your plans for the day should be the first thing you do in the morning and the last thing you do when you leave work at the end of the day. You still have over fifty-five hours of free time to spend as you please. Now let's take a look at how you can better use your work time.

Work Time

Many people complain of a lack of time to do all their daily business tasks. The best way to resolve this is to plan your days in advance, hour by hour, minute by minute, in blocks of time. By writing down how you plan to spend your day, you will instantly become far more productive. Since increased productivity means more money and greater success, it literally pays to use your time wisely. Time is the only thing you have to sell to your employer or business.

How much of the time you spend at work is really spent working? If you're like the average worker, very little of it is spent working effectively. Instead, you probably find your day filled with memo writing, paper shuffling, creative paper clip sculpting, and putting out fires.

Here is a simple and eye-opening way to see just how much work you really accomplish: Show up at work tomorrow with a stopwatch and a time management sheet with your day broken down into five-minute intervals. Keep the sheet and stopwatch with you at all times. As you start each new task write down what the task is and start your stopwatch. When you begin a different task (which includes being interrupted by phone calls or co-workers) write down the amount of time spent on the previous activity, then list the new activity and start your watch again.

At the end of the day take a separate piece of paper and write these four headings at the top:

1. Meaningful Work
2. Wasted Time (this includes interruptions and unimportant phone calls or discussions)
3. Problem Solving
4. Low Priority/Low Return Work

Underneath each of your headings list the appropriate tasks that you have dealt with that day, then add up the total time spent in each category. I'll bet you'll be shocked at just how little of your hours at work are spent on high priority, money making, or goal oriented tasks. Instead, you'll probably find that you spend an inordinate

amount of time looking for information, dealing with interruptions, and just plain wasting time.

DEVELOPING A TIME-EFFICIENT ENVIRONMENT

The first part of using your time profitably is to develop a
time-efficient environment at your home or office. This
means having all of your tools and resources in working
order and at hand. More time is lost because of inefficient
paper management and misplaced documents than because of any other cause. Make it a habit to keep your
work area and desk free of everything except the task at
hand. When you finish your work, immediately remove it,
mail it, file it, or trash it—whatever action is applicable.
Do not leave it on your desk.

One of the greatest time-savers ever invented is the filing cabinet. As soon as I finish a project I file it immediately.
When I am working on several projects at once I use baskets
to keep things separate. In the corner of my office I have two
sets of wire household baskets of the type used to store
sweaters. Each basket is labeled on the front with the project name. In them I keep all the books, reports, magazines,
articles, artwork, information, and other tools that relate to
that specific project. In this way all the tools I need to finish
a project are in one easily accessible place. As soon as the
project is over all the tools are immediately returned to
their respective shelves, boxes, or filing cabinets.

START EACH DAY WITH A CLEAR PLAN

I usually plan the next day's activities the night before. To do
this, use a sheet of paper or, better still, invest in a day planner. Write down all the tasks you want to complete tomor-

row. Then prioritize each task. The following day begin with the most important task and stick with it until you have finished it or reached the point that you wished to reach for that day. I derive a great sense of satisfaction in drawing a line through each task as I accomplish it. I'm sure you will too.

After developing an overall task list for the day I plan the day's specific activities in fifteen- to thirty-minute intervals using my daily planner. I even try to plan all of my meetings and phone calls. I set time limits on all meetings—especially with people who are not paying me for my time—and stick as close as possible to my timelines. If I schedule fifteen minutes to talk to advertising reps, I let them know that up front. They then make their points quickly and I save time. If necessary, as they near the end of their allotted time, I give them a two-minute warning. Then I try to bring the business to a close efficiently.

WRITE IT DOWN

Keep a pen and some paper by your phone. I can hardly believe the number of businesses I call only to be put on hold while they go off in search of a pen and paper. A pen and paper are the world's most essential business tools and you should never be without them.

Keep pen and paper by your bed, in your car, in your briefcase, in your jacket pocket, and on your desk. You just never know when a great idea is going to hit you. Great ideas are amazingly fleeting if not committed to paper.

I keep my appointment book open on my desk and when someone calls I make a note of why they called and how I am supposed to follow up. In this way I have a record of the time, date, and purpose of their call so I can refer to it later if necessary.

People are often surprised that I remember their names or the details of a conversation I had with them several months earlier, but it is as simple as writing it down initially, then flipping through my appointment book at a later date to look for the notes on our previous conversation. Also, I always write a person's phone number under their name so I never have to search further than my appointment book for names and numbers.

GET THE RIGHT TOOLS FOR THE JOB

Use whatever modern electronic aids you need to further your career and to make the most of your time. Get a car phone; get a fax; get a laptop computer; get a microrecorder for your home and office. Your investment in these tools will pay off rapidly in the form of increased productivity. If the cash expense is too high to buy them, then lease them. This equipment is as necessary as a car in today's business world.

I told a young women in one of my seminars that she ought to get a car phone. She replied that she wanted one but her company would not pay for it. "So what?" I countered. "If you buy one yourself, the time you save will increase your selling time and therefore your income dramatically. It will pay for itself." Why should she wait for her company to provide her with a car phone, even if she felt they should, when she could easily solve the problem herself? She got the point. Here was an example of a bright young woman putting the blame on someone else and not shouldering the responsibility herself.

DON'T WASTE YOUR TIME

Treat each minute as a valuable and precious resource. It is. Every person in this world starts out every day with the same amount of time in which to accomplish tasks and objectives. The only thing that differs from person to person is how that time is used. Successful people squeeze every second of opportunity from their day. Those at the lower levels simply waste it.

If you want to make $100,000 per year you must make $40 per hour. That is 66 cents per minute! If you spend twenty minutes on the phone talking to your buddy down the street about Monday night's football game, you have just wasted $13.20 of your valuable time. If you spend an extra half hour at lunch, you have just lost $19.80 of your time. Once lost, time can never be regained.

The next time you find yourself wasting time, ask yourself a question like this one: Would I pay my buddy down the street $13.20 in cold, hard cash, right now, out of my wallet, to listen to me talk about last night's game? The answer, of course, is no. Yet that is what you are doing. Wasting $13.20 of your cash, which should be dedicated to reaching your goals and serving your clients or business.

If you are working on a project and are interrupted by a call that takes ten minutes, it often takes another ten minutes to get back to what you were doing. Instead of being interrupted twenty times a day, schedule thirty minutes a day for returning phone calls that are not urgent. I always schedule my calls between 2 and 2:30 P.M. when people have returned from lunch.

When you receive calls from friends, salespeople, and others who are not clients, and who are keeping you from performing a business task, ask if they can call you back at a specified time or offer to return their call later. This helps you to avoid continual distractions from the unproductive phone calls. Your time at work is far too valuable for you to permit constant interruptions. Setting a specific time to call or be called back also eliminates playing phone tag.

Time Is Money

Take a look at the income you must make per month, week, hour, and minute to achieve your goals:

Year	Month	Week	Day	Hour	Minute
$150,000	$12,500	$2,884	$480	$60	$1.00
$100,000	$8,333	$1,923	$320	$40	$0.66
$90,000	$7,500	$1,730	$288	$36	$0.60
$80,000	$6,666	$1,538	$256	$32	$0.53
$70,000	$5,833	$1,346	$224	$28	$0.46
$60,000	$5,000	$1,153	$192	$24	$0.40
$50,000	$4,166	$961	$160	$20	$0.33
$40,000	$3,333	$769	$128	$16	$0.26

Note: Figures based on a fifty-two week, six day, forty-eight hour work week typical of most successful people.

If you want to make $100,000 a year, you must make $8,333 per month. This works out to be $1,923 per week based on a forty-eight hour, six day week. This breaks down further to $320 per day or $40 per hour.

Of course, you take time off and go on vacations. So the real figure is more like $50 per hour. But to keep it simple my calculations are based on forty-eight hours per week, fifty-two weeks a year. The table above is a powerful tool to help you reach your goals. It tells you exactly what you must make each and every hour in order to reach your desired income level. Now let's look at which of the tasks that you do during the day really produce $40 per hour.

- Advertising your business or yourself to others
- Selling products or selling yourself
- Increasing your inventory of skills
- Marketing yourself to others

These are tasks that really make $40 per hour. Good advertising makes the phone ring. Selling, whether it's a direct sale of your products or getting someone to give you an interview for a better job, definitely pays off. Increasing your inventory of skills makes you more valuable to yourself and to others and pays off quickly. Marketing keeps people involved in your life and brings in new contacts and prospects.

Now list five tasks specific to your profession that pay the amount of money you want to make.

1. _____
2. _____
3. _____
4. _____
5. _____

The following is a list of tasks that do not produce $40 per hour.

- Paying bills
- Ordering inventory
- Typing letters
- Adding to a database

I am not saying that these things are not important to the overall success of your business. Rather, I'm suggesting that you can find less qualified people to do these kind of tasks. These tasks can be done by others for just a few dollars an hour allowing you to focus on the high return tasks.

Make a list of the most time consuming tasks you do on a regular basis that are not worth $40 per hour (or whatever the per hour figure is for the income you desire).

1. _____
2. _____
3. _____
4. _____
5. _____

One of the toughest parts of running a business or of getting a promotion is that as you grow you must delegate more work to other people. This is tough because you worry that the work may not be done well and because you are giving up a certain amount of control. However, you must force yourself to use assistants to help you do less the important tasks so you can spend your time on more important ones. Make use of part-time help from your spouse or from a temporary service; you are helping yourself grow and prosper and you will quickly recoup the investment. You are also paving the road to help you reach your goals faster.

I have stressed throughout this book that you can reach your goals and that the principles of success are easy. And they are. They do, however, demand a great deal of self-discipline in order to make them work! Nowhere is this more apparent than in how you manage your time.

THE GREATEST WORD IN TIME MANAGEMENT

The simple act of saying "no" will save you more time, energy, and effort than you can possibly imagine. In an effort to try and please everyone we overextend ourselves taking on increased responsibilities and activities. These often overwork and stress us, causing irreparable harm rather than helping anyone. You know what I mean: Glenda calls and asks you to help out on the church fund-raising committee even though you already volunteer with the Cancer Society and the Rotary Club. Then Bob calls and asks if he can count on you to coach the little league team five nights a week even though you just finished the soccer season. And so it goes on and on. Demands on your time, energy, and effort. At some point you must say, "No. I am sorry but I can't." Try it; it's not that hard. And the people asking you will get over your refusal very quickly. In fact, they'll probably be dialing the next name on the list as soon as you hang up.

Put aside a set amount of time in your weekly plan to help your church, school, community, or friends. Once that time is used up it is gone and there is no more. Remember, in order to be successful you have to be ruthless about how you manage your time.

WHEN YOU DO TAKE TIME OFF, REALLY TAKE TIME OFF

Working hard is a prerequisite for making it big but you must also allow time off to recharge your batteries so you won't burn out. I play golf every Friday afternoon regardless of what happened in the office that week, of who wants to see me, or of what deals are pending. I get to the club early enough to hit balls and loosen up. When I play, I focus only on playing well and maybe winning a few bucks. I play with a group of fifteen to twenty other guys who make up the Friday Men's Club.

Several members of the group get there when I do. Some have lunch, some putt, and some just read the paper and have a beer. Others show up at the last minute, put their shoes on at the first tee, and eat lunch as they go down the first fairway. It takes them several holes before they settle into their game. By then both their score and their sanity hangs in the balance. To make matters worse a few of them stop at the pay phone on the eleventh tee to call up their offices and check on things one more time.

The problem is the eleventh is a tough par three over a large lake, requiring a well struck medium iron. Once off the phone with the rest of the day's problems at work fresh on their mind, how many of my associates do you think hit a good shot or even clear the lake? You're right. Not many.

Now their round and their peace of mind is well and truly destroyed.

If you are going to take time off work, take it and enjoy it! Leave your work at the office. When you go away on long weekends, forget work so completely that when you return to the office on Monday you feel like you have been gone for a month. You'll be far more productive. Give yourself some real time off and it will pay dividends.

Resolve now to be selective in how you spend your time at work. Do not waste it on tasks that do not pay you the money you should be earning. Find someone else to do the things that are less important. Focus your time on activities that help you reach your goals.

LESSON 5

INVEST IN YOUR
GREATEST ASSET

L et me ask you a very important question. How much are you worth? I don't mean how much do you wish you were getting paid. I mean, if you were your own boss what would you pay yourself based on your skills, talents, and performance? Would you give yourself a raise or a cut in pay?

Now most people would say that they should be making more money. But stop for a moment and put yourself in your boss's position. Look at your performance from his or her viewpoint and justify why you should be paid more. Almost everybody feels they are underpaid but just because someone else in the office is making more or because you show up on time everyday and nobody else does is not a good enough reason to justify a raise. Take a moment right now to list out the reasons why you should be paid more. Do it even if you are self-employed. For example, have you acquired additional experience that makes you worth more? Have you added to your inventory of skills by taking courses or reading books on your industry? Have you increased your sales or level of customer satisfaction?

Five Reasons I Deserve a Raise

1. _____
2. _____
3. _____
4. _____
5. _____

Now look at the reasons you came up with and ask yourself how many of them really merit a raise in pay. I am sure they are all good reasons, but are all five compelling? If you had trouble coming up with five truly outstanding reasons then you need to reevaluate your worth and take steps to improve it quickly. You must invest more time, money, and effort in your most important asset—yourself.

People often get themselves in a rut or a comfort zone where they don't want to change the way they do things because then they would have to invest a bit of effort to seek out new or better ways to run their business or their life. "After all," they reason, "my life is not that bad. I'm doing just fine." So they are, in effect, occupying a position in life that reflects the value of their present skills. They make about as much money as they are truly worth and they live their life accordingly. What about you? Are you living in the comfort zone? If you do not commit to upgrading your skills, you will become firmly stuck in a rut, watching as others race past you on the way to the top.

If you choose to invest in yourself your payoff will be both large and rapid simply because the majority of people never invest in themselves. For example, over 50 percent of the adult population in America reads less than one book per year. The last time most people entered a library was in college or high school. Many decide to stop learning when they get a specific promotion or have been in their present job for a few years. In fact, think of the number of people you have heard say, "I've been doing this job for twenty years." Apparently they are oblivious to the opportunities around them.

Today, technology grows at such a feverish pace that in order to stay at the top of your field you must double your knowledge every seven years. Nevertheless, the majority of the population stops trying to learn anything the moment they leave school—let alone trying to double their knowledge. This is, of course, a great shame because schools and colleges seldom offer more than a rudimentary coverage of the basic skills needed for success—if in fact they even offer that.

WHAT DO YOU FEED YOUR BRAIN?

What would happen to you physically if all you ate each day were large doughnuts filled with jelly? In addition, imagine you cut your exercise to zero, spent all day laying on the sofa, and drank only chocolate milk shakes? Within a very short period of time you would gain a huge amount of weight and be physically incapable of even simple cardiovascular activities. Your health would fail rapidly and eventually you would die.

If on the other hand you ate well-balanced meals each day, worked out regularly, and slept eight hours each night chances are you would probably live a long, healthy, and productive life. By investing in your body in the form of eating the right foods and exercising regularly you keep it in good shape.

So it is with your brain. If all you feed it are sitcoms, soap operas, dime novels, and sensational magazines you are giving it the equivalent of jelly doughnuts for food. If the only parts of the newspaper you read are the sports page and the cartoons you are giving your brain high fat chocolate milk that will put on mental pounds and slow you down.

There is a sign on the door of my dentist's office that says, "Ignore your teeth and they will just go away." The same is true of your brain. If you do not work it out by providing it with new and interesting material that will help you better your life you are simply letting it waste away. The less you stimulate your mind the less inclined it becomes to help you accomplish your goals. The more you stimulate your mind the more information it will crave and the faster and more substantial your progress will be.

THE UNIVERSITY OF YOU

The very fact that you are reading this book tells me that you are making an effort to upgrade your business and personal skills. You've made a great start, but don't let it end here. Put aside time each week to work out your mind just as you would your body. Read more books, attend seminars, and listen to audio tapes on a variety of topics that will aid you in your business and your life. The time and money you invest in the pursuit of knowledge will return to you a hundred times over—and far sooner than you thought possible.

Brian Tracy, president of Tracy Learning Systems, a company that specializes in human development, and author of many excellent audio programs, says that the single most valuable piece of advice he could ever give anyone is to invest 3 percent of their income in themselves. He maintains that people who follow this rule ultimately become the most successful people in their chosen field.

Life is too short to try to find all the answers for yourself. By drawing on the knowledge and experience of others you can shave months or even years off the time it takes you to achieve your goals and objectives. The more of this specialized, condensed knowledge you acquire the quicker you will move ahead. Here are my suggestions on how to educate yourself.

Audio Learning

Both the cassette player in your car and the ever increasing commute time to and from work offer an excellent opportunity to advance your knowledge every day. Invest in tape programs and audio seminars to augment your skills. I personally spend several hundred dollars each month to listen to the latest business, motivational, and biographical audio programs. There are also services available allowing you to rent books on tape at very reasonable rates through the mail. When you've finished a tape, you just send it back. Try turning off your radio for at least one leg of your daily journey (I find that morning is best since my mind is fresher) and stick in an audio tape.

Why not use your commute time to improve your skills in public speaking or time management or to increase your knowledge of health-related matters? How about mastering a second language or at least learning some conversational phrases to make your next vacation more enjoyable? Locals love to hear foreigners converse in their language. Try Spanish. It's virtually the official language in many parts of this country. Learning it may open up a whole new world of opportunity for your products and services.

Attend College in Your Car

Pick a specific area each month that you would like to improve and go to work on it. Let's say that this month you want to improve your planning ability. Get some tapes on time management, goal setting, or planning. Next month work on communications; the month after sales or negotiating. Look at the areas in your life which, if improved, would provide you with the greatest return. Then develop a course of study just like you'd have in a college semester, but with each month being a new term. Take one month to play the tapes repeatedly until you have mastered the concepts they contain. If you follow this simple method, at the end of the year you will have significantly increased your knowledge in twelve specific areas. And if you choose the tapes wisely you will have learned far more than if you had attended a full-time college. At a fraction of the cost in time or money, too!

Audio programs that I recommend include those by Earl Nightingale, Brian Tracy, Ken Blanchard, Anthony Robbins, Dale Carnegie, and Tony Vercillo. Use these successful people to spur you on to your goals. Think of these programs as being your own personal success trainers.

Although not as convenient because they must be viewed with a television, videos offer an excellent and highly visual way to improve your skills. You can improve your golf or tennis game, take in someone's life story, or improve your sales skills.

Since the variety and depth of audiovisual information available today is overwhelming, be sure to stay on track. Select the programs that are most likely to move you toward your goals. With so much quick and valuable information available, it is easy to become an information junkie shooting through one program and then racing off in search of the next. Develop an action notebook in the back of your daily planner to jot down new concepts and ideas. Then use your planning time at the end of the day to transfer these thoughts into action strategies to be implemented by you before you seek more information. After each tape series or seminar, take some kind of specific action before you seek out new ideas. Then by all means seek out more!

Seminars

Seminars offer perhaps the best method of gaining specific knowledge quickly and easily. They provide the opportunity to learn firsthand from an expert in a specific subject or field who has spent many years refining the information to its very essence. This not only provides you with a very concentrated presentation but it also spares you a great deal of time in trying to find the information by yourself. Live seminars allow you to get valuable feedback from the speaker. You can ask questions and probe deeper into those areas that interest you most. Often you will find that other people ask excellent questions, questions about problems you have not yet considered. This type of interaction leads to the creation of other ideas and questions that can be asked and answered at a seminar. This gives you the most complete and personally customized information available.

A side benefit of attending such seminars is that the people who attend will often share some of your visions and dreams. This makes seminars an excellent place to meet others with whom to develop business or personal relationships.

Read Biographies

If there is one activity that I rate above all others it is reading. You can learn more in a few hours from a good book than you can in a year of trial and error. A Gallup survey of people listed in *Who's Who* found that over 80 percent of those surveyed read a great deal. Fortunately, I developed a love of reading from my parents around the time I was ten years old. From that point on I read as much as I could get my hands on. I read the fabulous stories of suspense and intrigue by Alistair MacLean, Hammond Innes, Frederick Forsyth, Willbur Smith, and

others. I sat up all night without sleeping to finish reading
Peter Benchley's Jaws. In short, I developed a passion for
reading.

As life gets busier and more complicated there seems
to be less time to read, but I urge you to find the time to
rediscover the wonder of reading. Always keep a business
book or magazine in your car. Always keep one in your
briefcase so you can catch up on ten or fifteen minutes of
reading while you are waiting for an appointment. Always
carry reading material when you go for lunch alone, when
you have to stand in line for something, or when you take
a cab. You will be surprised how this spare time can be
turned into productive reading time.

Read the biographies of famous and influential people
like Churchill, Roosevelt, Lincoln, Einstein, Edison, and
Ford. From them you will glean a vast amount of knowledge. Their lives and successes will give you reference
points on key decisions they made that may well pay off in
your business or personal life. By looking at the actions
and decisions that changed history you can often find answers to your own problems.

General George Patton studied the wars and battles
of ancient Rome and Greece as well as those of Napoleon
in order to defeat Rommel during World War II. The past
will also offer you solutions to the problems you face today.

Not only will biographies help you solve problems but
they will also motivate you to greater things as you learn
of the huge setbacks that many successful people over-
came in order to achieve greatness. Biographies can thus
be both informative and motivational. And the knowledge
you gain of the lives of famous people also makes great
material for starting conversations and developing rapport with others.

Reading has changed the lives of millions of people
around the world. A small boy from Independence, Mis-
souri, was given a book for his tenth birthday entitled
Great Men and Famous Women. President Harry Truman

would later say that reading that book was one of the turning points of his life. His love of books prompted him and a friend to announce that they would both read all two thousand books in the public library—encyclopedias and all—and they did.

Business Books Open New Doors

You can improve your knowledge of any subject a thousand times over simply by reading a book on it. Even if you are already well versed in a certain subject reading a book on it is almost certain to give you additional ideas and information. Read books on specific skills that are used in your job. Not only will it increase your business knowledge but it will often open your eyes to new and more interesting possibilities in your life. It did with me.

While in college I took an advertising course because I thought it would be very interesting. It turned out to be awful. It offered no useful information and every test we took was based strictly on terminology. None of it had anything to do with creating copy, graphics, and designs that actually sold products. The class was so bad that it almost killed my interest in the subject forever. It took something of a crisis to renew it.

When I moved to California and began running my karate school I quickly became frustrated by the poor return that my ads were getting. I was not receiving enough phone calls from each ad to pay for the ad itself—let alone increase my business. At first I turned for help to the advertising representatives from the newspapers in which my ads where running. After all, didn't their living depend on helping people get results? Surely they would know how to increase my response. Wrong! They were so ill informed of the basic concepts of advertising that talking to them was nothing short of pathetic. On one occasion a rep pulled out an ad that was used by a florist up the street.

She said that they received a good response from that particular layout and that I ought to do my ad the same way. (It is truly amazing to me that in all the small businesses I have run I have never met a newspaper advertising representative that knew the first thing about advertising. Had any of them taken the slightest effort to understand basic headline, copy, and layout rules they could have instantly improved their clients' response and made selling them an ad so much easier next time around. Alas, that would have meant spending twenty dollars of their own money and wasting their precious weekend reading!)

It was obvious that the only thing that concerned my local paper was selling me space and nothing more, so I set about finding out the information I needed for myself. I went to the local bookstore and bought every book they had on advertising—about five or six. I then bought some trade magazines and through them ordered another ten books. I read books on copy, design, layout, direct mail, media planing, public relations, and common mistakes in advertising. I also read several biographies on the top people in the business like David Ogilvy. I read each book armed with a yellow highlighter. I circled, underlined, and copied the key points in each book. Within a matter of weeks I had discovered most, if not all, of the main principles of good advertising.

I took these principles and applied them to the advertising for my karate studio. Instantly the phone started ringing off the hook. The first week I ran my new ad I signed up eighteen new members in just four days, bringing in over five thousand dollars from a three hundred dollar ad in my local paper.

By taking the time to read up on advertising I vaulted my business almost overnight to the top of its field. These simple actions were the major reason for my rapid success in the karate business and I was well on my way to making over $100,000 a year despite being just twenty-five years old.

I was also on my way to a dual career. As I will tell you later, action—any kind of action—also creates opportunity. I had read so many books on the subject and had became so fascinated with advertising that I began my own advertising agency. I built a small office in the back of my karate school, bought a computer, and some artwork, and went to work. At first I did ads for other karate studios and martial arts supply stores. Soon I was designing ads for other businesses in my business center. Then for local restaurants and other small businesses. Within twelve months I had acquired several national advertising accounts and had hired a full-time copywriter, an artist, and a typesetter.

I learned advertising from books. I never worked for an agency or took any other courses except the dismal college course I mentioned earlier and yet within a few weeks I had first class knowledge. I know it was first class because it got instant results both for my business and for the companies that hired me. When I wrote my first book, I was able to sell over $150,000 worth of books in just twelve months entirely through my own direct marketing efforts.

It is amazing how quickly and extensively you can increase your knowledge of any subject just by reading books. You can become an expert in almost any area simply by finding out which are the best books on any given subject and then reading them carefully. The best part of it all is you don't even have to pay for them; you can go to your library and get them for free.

If you dislike your present job or business go out today and pick up a book on a business or career that is of interest to you. Read it from cover to cover then go back and get another one, then another. Within a few weeks you will have a basic knowledge of the industry's terminology and workings. From that point you can make an evaluation of what to do next. Did the books you read discourage you from moving into this field? Or did they excite you to take further action and find out more practical knowledge on the subject?

Picking up a book offers you an immediate, practical, and private way to increase your knowledge of any subject you choose. Instead of wishing you had paid more attention in high school, gone to college, studied harder, or finished your MBA, go out and get a book. The information you seek can be found within its pages.

Read Magazines

With the fast pace of today's world it is essential that you stay up on the new trends in your industry. The easiest way to accomplish this is to read magazines of interest to your career and personal life. Pay special attention to trade magazines, booklets, and newsletters. They contain the most up to date and potentially useful information.

You might also invest some time in reading magazines that are of no particular interest to you but are greatly interesting to your boss or to a major client. Read about gardening, business, golf, football, cooking, running, finance, clothing—whatever it takes. The broader your range of knowledge, the better. Think of it as being armed for war with every type of weapon that you might need in case of action.

Make it a habit to visit a bookstore at least twice a month. Invest in various books and magazines, covering a wide range of material. Read them for content and make notes on what you've read. Review these notes as required, particularly prior to big meetings or social events, thus keeping the information fresh in your mind. Remember, information by itself is not powerful. Information put into action is powerful.

Take Classes

Expand your knowledge of interesting subjects by enrolling in a night class. Most night school courses are taught by people who either work professionally in the field on which they teach or who have other firsthand experience. This often makes these courses far more valuable than a similar college course taught by a teaching professional who may or may not have had any real-world experience. Many schools now offer these courses early in the morning before work, in the evenings, and on weekends so there is no excuse not to make the time to attend.

Take a class in using computers! You won't go wrong in this day and age by learning more about computers and the programs they run. And remember my suggestion to learn a foreign language via an audio tape? Well, perhaps you learn better in a classroom environment. Pick up a second language at the local community college. Also, look into courses on retirement planning, investing, or money management so you will be able to handle your money correctly when its flow increases dramatically.

WHAT TYPE OF INFORMATION WILL MOVE YOU AHEAD THE FASTEST?

I have discussed the various forms of gathering information and adding to your personal inventory of skills, but which specific skills will pay you the greatest dividend? That depends on your specific career and background but I can recommend three important areas that if neglected will curtail success.

The first is to improve your ability to manage time. After all, as Ben Franklin said, "That is the very stuff of which life is made." The second area is to improve your communication and sales skills whether or not you actually sell a product for a living. The third is to gain the greatest amount of knowledge about your actual product, business, or job that is possible. Leave no stone unturned in your effort to learn everything you possibly can.

Reading and taking courses are an excellent start in your investment in yourself. Often these actions may deliver sufficient information for you to act, but if not try some of the following ways to invest in your future.

DON'T FORGET ON-THE-JOB TRAINING

The finest way to get reliable information of any kind is firsthand. No other method offers more accurate training on how a business or service should be run than by actually working in that business with a successful company. Many of this country's tycoons built great fortunes by thoroughly learning a job through working for others. They then branched out on their own.

Many airline pilots are selected from the ranks of the military where they received their on-the-job training. Most advertising agencies are started by a small staff who gained a great deal of experience from an agency then left to set up their own shop. On-the-job training allows you to go into a project with your eyes open. It exposes you to the possibilities and dangers of any venture.

Ninety percent of all small businesses in this country fail in their first year. This is largely due to the owners having a lack of knowledge in key subjects such as advertising, management, and sales. Worse still, many businesses fail before they ever open their doors because they are begun by people who know little or nothing about the industry. Blinded by the lure of "hassle-free" income or the quick talk of a salesman they invest in laundromats, dry cleaners, and video stores. It soon becomes clear that the business is far from being hassle free and farther still from being profitable.

If your small town doesn't have a hamburger joint and you want to open one, take some lessons. First, get a job with someone who has done it well. Work behind the counter or, better still, become the manager of a McDonalds or Burger King. In just a few months you will learn how to run a hamburger business from people who have made a science out of doing it. Spend six months. You may decide that it is not really what you want to do, in which case you will have saved yourself a great deal of time, effort, and money. On the other hand you may feel even better about the business, and now your chances of success are immeasurably better than they were a few months ago. You have invested in yourself and received a short, simple, and incredibly practical education that cannot be beat.

ASK A WINNER HOW HE WON

A great way to gain valuable firsthand information is to seek out others who have been successful in your field and to ask them for advice. As the saying goes, the best thing a poor man can do is to take a rich man to lunch. Once at the table pick their brains for every morsel of information that may help you. Find out what made this person successful so that you can follow the same course of action. Contrary to a widely held belief, successful people are often very amenable to this type of conversation and there are several good reasons.

First, successful people are *people* and they enjoy talking about themselves and their achievements—it's just human nature. Ask a winner how he won and he will be glad to tell you in as much detail as you can bear to hear. Second, successful people like to share their success with others. They are more than happy to give people a ride on their coattails. It's one of the rewards of success. Third, because of their success, many people are intimidated by them and so they are approached far less often than you would think with this type of proposition.

Find people locally who can offer you a great deal of advice, introduce yourself to them, tell them that you admire their work, then ask them out for breakfast, lunch, or a drink after work. It works! And it also brings us to the next valuable way to increase your knowledge.

FIND ROLE MODELS

It is not necessary for you to have access to successful people in your field in order to use them as role models. If you pick a person who has reached the top and do exactly what he or she did in order to get there, your chances of obtaining the same results will increase dramatically. People who reach the top do so because they have developed a specific range of talents, thoughts, and actions. Their success is nothing more than the result of this trio. If you cultivate the same talents, think in the same way, and take the same actions your chances of succeeding will be greatly enhanced.

What makes a particular person successful? What key facets can be identified and reduced to their simplest forms? Let's take a look at someone famous, someone you will have seen on television and read about. See if you agree with the points I make.

Lee Iacocca became president of Ford Motor Company at age thirty-six. He dreamed up the Ford Mustang, which sold like no other car ever had and he later brought the Chrysler Corporation back from bankruptcy. What are the reasons he became so successful? Here are a few suggestions.

1. He had a *passion* in life: He loved cars, loved the auto business, and loved what he was doing. That in itself is a great start toward living a successful life.

2. He had excellent *communication skills*. Another prerequisite for reaching the top of almost any field.

ро .

3. He *listened* to what people wanted and then gave it to them. The huge popularity of the Mustang proves this fact. He listened for a need and then filled it.

4. He had his own *role models* and garnered from them a wealth of knowledge.

5. He had excellent *sales skills*. This not only sold his company and his products but it also sold him.

6. He *dressed well*. He looked the part of a successful corporate executive.

7. He *sought the very best people* to help him in his tasks. He was not afraid to hire people who were smarter than him.

8. He was *resilient*. When he was fired from Ford, he hung in and eventually returned in triumph.

As a point of interest I have never met Lee Iacocca, although I would like to. I have gained this insight into him by reading his biography and newspaper articles about him, by listening to his speeches, and by seeing him on television. The point is you don't need to know someone personally in order to have him or her as a role model. You just need to recognize them as successful and then investigate as many sources as necessary to find out why. The examples I have just provided regarding Lee Iacocca are short and simple. The real list you would develop would of course be much longer and comprise both significant and seemingly insignificant items.

Some of the things that you might identify in your personal role model, such as an advanced education, will take time for you to acquire for yourself, especially if you can only do so on weekends and in the evenings. Other factors will be very easy to emulate, for example dressing well. Being a good listener is also a simple trait you can develop if you consciously set out to develop that character quality. Just because a trait is seemingly insignificant and easy to emulate does not make it any less a piece of the puzzle of success. Do not discount these simple and easy to acquire items. Instead, start investing in your future by applying them now. After all, since they are so simple they will take very little effort. But they will pay off well in the end.

Whom Should You Pick as a Role Model?

Their are literally millions of people who would make excellent role models. Still, let's look at a few ways to determine the best possible role model to help you in your present situation. First, pick someone who has made it on their own not someone who has inherited wealth and power, unless of course he or she has taken what was received to significantly greater heights. Pick someone who started a successful company. Someone who builds a successful business from the ground up must know a thing or two about how to get to the top.

Second, pick someone who excels in a line of work or career similar to yours. Selecting Michael Jordan as a role model will yield some examples in terms of commitment and dedication, but he is not your ideal role model if you work for an oil company in Alaska and dream of someday owning your own well.

Third, look for someone whose life appears to be in balance. Do not pick a rock star who is constantly in trouble with drugs, alcohol, women, and the police—unless, of course, that is what you really want. Pick someone who is successful not only monetarily but also in relationships and dealings with others.

A good example of a person who has matched his desires and talents well toward a specific and lofty goal is Bill Clinton. Ever since his early teens his role model has been John F. Kennedy. He hoped someday to be one of the youngest presidents in history; obviously having Kennedy as a role model helped him. Clinton is also a good example of how no matter how far up the ladder of success you climb there is always room for a role model in your life.

Choosing Your Own Role Models

Is there someone now in your line of work or at your office who is particularly successful and who you admire? It does not matter if you have never met the person nor if you are ever likely to meet. Pick someone right now for the purpose of this exercise and list ten reasons why you think this person is so successful. Remember, the reasons can be either significant or seemingly insignificant.

1. _____
2. _____
3. _____
4. _____
5. _____
6. _____
7. _____
8. _____
9. _____
10. _____

Now look at your list. How many of this person's key reasons for success do you presently possess? How many of them could you acquire over the next year? Over the next five years? Which of these traits is the most important? Prioritize the traits on your list. Now start work today on developing the most important trait.

List ten things you could do now to invest in yourself and develop or improve your present skills, such as studying Spanish, learning to use computers, or developing better time management skills.

1. _____
2. _____
3. _____
4. _____
5. _____
6. _____
7. _____
8. _____
9. _____
10. _____

Now list five opportunities or positive events that may appear because you have invested in yourself in the ways you have listed above.

1. _____
2. _____
3. _____
4. _____
5. _____

When are you going to start investing in your most important asset? Why not start today! Go out and buy another book.

Resolve now to upgrade your business training and skills. Attend seminars, read books, and listen to audio tapes. If you do, you will always be in the top 5 percent of people in your chosen field.

LESSON 6

GETTING THE MOST IMPORTANT PERSON IN THE WORLD TO HELP YOU

I n order to make it big you need the help of others. You need people who will lend you money, who will work with you, and who will help you reach your goals. If they do not directly aid your cause, then you need them to do it indirectly as a customer who buys your products or services. In short, your ability to communicate with others directly affects your chances of success.

Getting others to do as you want whether you pay them or not is essential to your success. Even in a well-disciplined army it is the generals with the best people skills who enter the history books. It's not the ones who shout the loudest.

THE MOST IMPORTANT PERSON IN THE WORLD

Enlisting people in your army is easy. All you need to know to make it happen is the answer to one simple question:

103

Who is the most important person in the world? Of course the answer most people will give is the president, a religious leader, a scientist, an athlete, or an entertainer. What is your answer?

The correct answer is obvious. To 99.99 percent of the world's population, the most important person in the world is *them*. The prospect, customer, friend, or foe you are speaking to at any given moment is the most important person in the world—at least to them.

It is amazing that so few people ever grasp this simple fact of life. I know it took me a lot longer than it should have. It seems that this realization is one of those that comes only with age and experience and even then it often eludes all but the most astute. It came to Lincoln in his thirties when, after writing a scathing editorial of a prominent local in a newspaper, his subject challenged him to a duel to the death. Fortunately for Lincoln and the rest of America the duel was stopped at the last second when friends of the two men intervened. From that point on Lincoln found better, more diplomatic ways of letting people know that he did not agree with their point of view.

No matter what your age, pay close attention to this chapter. If you learn the following principles they will be some of the most important lessons of your life. The sooner you apply them the sooner they will bring you handsome rewards. It is never too late to get people on your side, and the results of doing so are always the same. You will reach your goals a lot faster.

WHAT'S IN IT FOR ME?

With rare exception, people are not interested in you or what you did for someone else. They are only interested in what you can do for them. A walking example of this principle is the advertising representative who called on me at my karate school and tried to sell me his services. As soon as he entered my office he began telling me about all the wonderful things he had done for a competitor in the martial arts business. He was still talking when I showed him the door. Of course he never got my business. Why? He never stopped talking long enough about what he had done for my competitor to find out that I deliberately followed a course of action directly opposite from theirs.

Each person you meet has a deep subconscious desire to be treated like the most important person in the world. A person's highest need is to be respected and recognized. If you let someone down in this regard, you will lose a sale, a prospect, or a friend.

GO AHEAD—MAKE THEIR DAY

Set a goal to make as many people as possible feel great each and every time you come into contact with them. Build them up, compliment them at every opportunity, and make them feel great about themselves and about their relationship with you. You will be rewarded a hundredfold for your effort and it really doesn't take much. Rid yourself of negative comments and make today the day you start talking positively to those around you. Talk only in terms of the things you like and admire about people and let others dish out the criticism.

It is very easy to forget how the simple things in life can contribute dramatically to people's perception of you and how much they can add to your chances of success. One day, I was standing in the lobby of one of my karate studios when an attractive middle-age mother brought in her son for his lesson. I happened to be wearing a blue sweater that day, and as she stooped briefly in front of me she said, "You have the most beautiful blue eyes. You should wear blue more often." She said it with sincerity and with no other purpose than to compliment me. I walked on air the rest of the day! I felt great! I looked at myself in the mirror and admired my blue eyes! Later that night I reflected on my day and I thought of what a silly thing it was that this simple comment could actually make my day. Here I was young, healthy, successful, and happy—my life was great—and yet this simple comment made it even better.

I began to wonder what effect the same type of sincere compliment would have on people who attended my studios. Some of them had just spent three hours fighting traffic on the freeway after a hard day's work. Perhaps their boss had been criticizing them all day. They faced overdue bills, sick kids, flat tires, speeding tickets, and all the other ins and outs of daily life. If this simple act of kindness worked on me, someone who had few problems in the world, surely it would meet with even greater success when applied to others who needed the boost far more. I decided to put it into action the very next day. It worked wonderfully! From that point on I resolved to make at least three people's day every day with a simple and sincere comment on something I liked about them.

In the bank I would comment on a pretty sweater or dress. At my business I would compliment a customer's new car or truck. In restaurants or on the phone I would mention how happy or enthusiastic the people I dealt with sounded. The effect was astonishing; people with whom I had exchanged only a few words went out of their way to help me. Bartenders offered me free drinks; at self-service gas stations people would wash my windows. My staff began to work harder and with renewed enthusiasm knowing that their effort would not escape my newly trained eye which sought out every opportunity for praise.

I was in Philadelphia recently at a seminar. I stopped in the hotel restaurant for breakfast. They had a buffet bar at which a huge chef was cooking omelets. I ordered a veggie omelet full of onions, tomatoes, cheese, and mushrooms. The chef took obvious care in making it and it was quite simply one of the best omelets I have ever eaten.

After breakfast I went over to where the chef had been cooking omelets to thank him. He was nowhere to be seen so I wandered into the kitchen. When he turned around and saw me he was startled, but his look of surprise turned into one of the biggest grins I have ever seen when I told him how much I enjoyed his omelet.

Keep your eyes and ears open to what is going on around you and learn to spot what others are interested in and proud of. If you hear that a friend has a new car, or you notice it yourself, ask if you can take a closer look. Your friend will be delighted that you noticed and that you are interested in both him and his car. When you see it, comment on something you like about its appearance. "That's a beautiful shade of blue. What do they call it?" or "Great looking stereo system. I bet it sounds great." Then take a couple of minutes out of your busy day to let him show it off. This will make your friend feel great. Knowing that you like his car is like a vote of personal approval for him. It builds his self-confidence and self-esteem and it makes him feel like a million bucks. Simple attention shown to others pays off with customers, family, and friends.

Notice the women in your life. Tell them how nice their new dress looks or that their hairstyle really suits them. Comments like these pay off tenfold. I am not suggesting that you tell people things you do not mean or that you should be insincere. On the contrary, if you are not sincere, it will surely backfire on you. People are very astute in spotting insincerity. Instead, pay as much attention to other people as you do to yourself. Paying attention to other people and the things that matter to them will pay dividends when you need something in return.

The easiest way to make people instantly like you is to show a genuine interest in them and the things that they like. Instead of talking about all the things you have done encourage them to tell you about themselves. Help people open up to you and then listen to what they have to say. Have you heard the old saying as to why God gave you two eyes, two ears, and only one mouth? Well, it wasn't so you could talk up a storm. Using your eyes and ears when first meeting a person can be pivotal in the success of the relationship.

REMEMBER PEOPLE'S NAMES

Remembering a person's name is one of the sincerest compliments you can pay them. It builds their self-esteem by telling them that they have made an impression on you and that they are important to you. The sound of a person's name, said correctly, is to them one of the nicest sounds in the world.

Do you doubt this? Think about how you felt when someone sent you a letter and horribly misspelled your name. Did it leave you impressed with the writer and his or her abilities? Not likely. Instead you probably shook your head, rolled your eyes, and muttered under you breath. The same is true when someone verbally butchers your name.

It is vital when you engage in a conversation or are introduced to people that you remember their name. The fastest way to lose the rapport you are building is to forget their name and have to ask it again. It has been shown that calling someone by their name, first or last, dramatically increases bonding among those communicating. People feel like they know you if you call them by a familiar name.

Some people are good with names—virtually everyone who is successful! President Harry Truman could call literally thousands of people, from senators to scullery maids, by their first name. Can you imagine how you would feel if the president of the United States called you by your first name? Can you imagine the lengths staff members might go to if the president took the trouble to remember their names? If you improve your ability to remember people's names you will soon discover the astonishing power of this simple act.

If you make the effort to correctly pronounce the name of someone with an unusual or foreign name it is a hundred times more impressive to them. If you work at correctly saying a particularly difficult name you may be the only person who has ever made the effort. That makes for a powerful bond in your relationship that will have very deep roots. Who wouldn't like and respect you when you alone went to the trouble of learning to pronounce their name correctly?

Unfortunately, not everyone has a photographic memory to instantly put a name to a face. To remember names or other data the first time you hear them, you must pay attention. Be really mentally alert when you are introduced to new people. Listen closely for names and repeat them silently several times. If you are unsure that you heard a name correctly, ask for it to be repeated. Ask for the pronunciation again if it is unusual. If necessary repeat the name back in a way that encourages correction: "Nice to meet you—Darin?" Or just echo the name to acknowledge that you heard it: "Nice to meet you, Darin." Use their name as often as you can in the first minute you talk to them and look directly at them; this will help you reinforce both their name and their face.

Some memory techniques tell you to look at the person's face and link a facial feature with the sound of the name. For example, remember "Rosie" by picturing giant roses on her cheeks or "Mike" by seeing a large microphone jutting from his strong jaw. The idea is to look for a facial feature and link their name with that feature. This technique greatly improves your name retention ability.

Another technique is to link the new person to a person you know well. For example, if I meet a "Ron" I link him to my good friend Ron. I find something that is similar with the new Ron and associate it with the familiar Ron. This way your mind links the two people and their names together, thus making forgetting difficult.

These techniques will greatly assist you in remembering the names and faces of new people. They will also facilitate bonding with these people quickly and completely. Meeting new people will become fun and rewarding.

USE YOUR EYES

Once you have initially established contact and got the persons name it is time to put your eyes to work to search for common ground that will aid you in building rapport. When you meet someone in their office or home look for the things that are important to them. If you see a civic award or a picture of the person with someone famous, immediately ask for more details: "When did you meet so and so? What kind of person were they?" The floodgates of conversation will burst open. People display such pictures and awards because they are proud of them. If they weren't, why would they hang them on the wall? They want people to take notice of what important people they are to have earned such awards and mingled with such interesting people.

Look for pictures of family and friends, dogs, fishing trips, golf tournaments, charity events—anything that would give you clues to their underlying interests. Dead giveaways are trophies or golf, tennis, or fishing paraphernalia. Trinkets on desks and shelves that would give you a clear indication of a person's hobbies include paperweights, football helmets, or a horse's head pen set. Look for the presence of books that might help you. Are there books on aviation, sailing, or painting?

When I was working as a waiter while in college the other waiters couldn't believe how I could instantly spot a golfer. Well, I had a system. First I looked for a shirt with a country club logo or name on it. Then I looked for the Izod crocodile shirt that most golfers of that time wore. In the absence of these telltale signs I looked at their left hand to see if a golf glove had kept it a lighter shade than their right hand in the bright Florida sun. If these signs were absent I would simple listen to their conversation. If they were golfers the conversation would quickly reveal the fact. I would then jump in and ask a couple of well-chosen questions. The end result? I'd always bring in higher tips at the end of the night.

HOW TO START A CONVERSATION

People are more than happy to tell you what they like if you only provide the opportunity for them to do it. Encourage them to talk about themselves and their interests while you listen. You can stimulate this type of communication by asking questions that cannot be answered by yes or no, by asking questions that are not threatening, and by asking questions that allow people to talk about themselves. Consider asking the following opening questions:

"What type of work do you do?"

"How did you get into your line of work?"

"What are your hobbies?"

"Where are you from?"

More specific openings are:

"Your dress is very attractive. What do they call that shade?"

"Where did you purchase your dress?" (This question allows you to discuss the type of shop she purchased

it from and could lead to all kinds of good questions—
then, bingo! you're having a conversation!)

"I see you know the waiter very well. What's the best dish
on the menu?" (This is a compound question but helps to
ensure that you don't get just a yes or no answer.)

Once you get an opening question answered, use the
information you received to form the next question. The
general rule of thumb is to get them talking about themselves (i.e., where they work, where they live, how long
have they been in the city or state, where were they born,
why they came here). Once you have them talking, encourage them to keep talking about themselves. This will
give you the time to analyze the person and to establish
grounds for further conversation.

LEARN FROM A PERSON'S CHOICE OF WORDS

You can gain a great deal of insight into a person from the
words they use. This can be extremely useful when you
are trying to get them on your side and to agree with your
point of view. When talking to people listen carefully to the
way they describe things. Do they talk in terms of strikeouts and home runs or do they speak of first downs and
scoring touchdowns? These are, of course, very obvious examples but if you listen a little more closely you will be
surprised at how quickly you can zone in on a person's particular interests.

Once you have a conversation going on a subject that
interests the person, listen attentively to how they use
key words in their description of events. How they talk to
you can also tell you a great deal about how they process
the information you give them.

Have you ever been in a meeting or conversation
with someone that you really wanted to hear but you just

could not connect with anything they said? On the other hand, have you ever dreaded talking to someone only to find that you seemed to be on the same wavelength and you grew to like them very quickly? People tend to share and process information in a few different ways, and if you happen to match communication styles you'll find that you communicate well. If, however, your communication styles are at odds, you'll have a tough time getting into the conversation.

Essentially people process information in one of three ways: visually, aurally, and kinesthetically. Visually oriented people talk in terms of what they see. People with an aural orientation talk of what something sounds like. Kinesthetic people are into what they feel. If you know how a particular person processes information you can tailor the way you talk to them and have a better chance of getting your points across. For example, ask a friend to tell you about their vacation in Hawaii and you will hear variations of these three descriptions.

"It was great. The sand was a brilliant white and the water was a perfect blue–green. There were huge mountains with lush green plants that came down almost to the water's edge."

"It was absolutely great! I felt so relaxed there. The water was warm and the air was full of the smell of tropical plants. That place just felt great. I think I want to move there."

"Just listen to this: We went scuba diving at Hanauma Bay and heard the porpoises. You should have heard what my wife said after that."

Okay, you have read three descriptions of Hawaii. What type of person would have used the first type of description: visual, aural, or kinesthetic? What about the second? The third?

If you said the order was visual, kinesthetic, and aural you are right. So how does this make a difference to you? Well, it makes a big difference in terms of getting the most from your communications.

Visual People

The visual group of people are those who can watch an event and then perform it with few errors. They are people who learn by watching. They learn best from watching TV or reading books. When they recall data from their mind, they first see it in pictures and then use these pictures to recall the desired data.

Kinesthetic People

These people learn by touching or by using their sense of feel. In contrast to visuals, they process information by developing a sense of rhythm, flow, and feel.

Aural People

Aural people process data via hearing or listening to what people say. These people will stand and listen to what you have to say. They then process the input mentally and proceed accordingly.

It is important to understand the type of person you are working with. This will lead to faster, more efficient, and easier communication. For example, suppose two equally skilled people develop an identical computer problem. They both phone technical support to get the problem fixed, but one person takes three minutes to apply the solution while the second person takes twenty.

The next day another problem arises but a representative of the software company happens to be in the building and offers to help. He logs on the computer with the first person and goes through the steps needed to correct the problem three times. The second person picks it up the first time. This is an example of what happens when a person's own communication style differs from that of the person he is trying to communicate with.

The first person responded better to aural communication, therefore when he called for support over the phone he quickly got the answers he needed and solved the problem. When he had to sit down and watch someone show him how to do it, he found it much harder. The second person was visually oriented so while the telephone call profited her little, being able to watch the problem being fixed enabled her to quickly grasp the solution.

Some people like to be shown things, others like to be told things, while still others need to experience and feel things before they are convinced. By paying careful attention to which way a person appears to respond best you can modify your approach so that your words fit with the words the other person uses. This will develop rapport quickly and will greatly enhance your chances of building a lasting relationship.

Let's play a little game. Write the names of five people who are important to you and with whom you communicate often. For example, your boss, your wife, your staff.

1. _____

2. _____

3. _____

4. _____

5. _____

Now listen very carefully to each of these people today and try to discover the way in which each takes in and processes information. Here are some key words to help you with this task.

Visual

- Picture this
- Can you see my point?
- Let me show you how
- Imagine this

Aural

- Listen
- Do you hear what I'm saying?
- Does this click?
- Is he in tune with us?

Kinesthetic

- It doesn't feel right
- Can you grasp what I am saying?
- Are you catching on now?

Playing this little game is fun and with the information it provides you can do a great deal to quickly improve your communication skills. Once you have discovered into which group each person falls start to use their type of key words and phrases when you are interacting with them.

If you are a visual person and are talking to someone who appears to be aurally inclined, avoid talking in visual terms. Do not say, "Hank, picture this." Hank is not going to picture it the way you do. Instead say, "Hank, listen to this." Then carefully describe your plan to him.

Develop Active Listening Techniques to Increase Rapport

Standing in front of a person and looking in their general direction does not guarantee good communication even if you are listening attentively to what he or she has to say. It is important that you practice "active listening" to convince your speaker that you are indeed attentive and interested. This is a method of listening to people and giving them the encouraging feedback that facilitates good communication and puts the other person at ease.

The first technique in this method is to establish eye contact and hold it. Have you ever talked to a person who didn't look at you or who was always looking around? How did it make you feel? Isn't it uncomfortable to talk with a person who doesn't appear to be interested in what you are saying? A person who consciously or subconsciously isn't interested in what you have to say will look away frequently, signaling that you are not important enough to pay attention to. It's a form of rejection. Therefore make sure that you do not do this to other people. Make eye contact with your speaker, look at his or her face, and hold this posture during the conversation. This communicates that you are interested in the subject material and in the speaker.

The second technique is to give feedback throughout the conversation. As a person speaks, use words like, "I agree," "Yes," "I see," or "Interesting." These words are a form of verbal "eye contact," providing approval without stopping the conversation. Speaking of stopping a conversation, have you ever had people cut you off just to start talking about themselves? It stifles rapport. Make sure you don't do it to those with whom you are talking.

Effective communication takes practice; do not confuse opening your mouth with communication. The actual physical act of speaking is just a small part of the total communications picture. The strategies I have just discussed go a long way toward making up the rest of the picture and it pays to employ them with everyone you meet. You just never know who people are or who they might know until you have spoken to them for a few minutes. For this reason you must know the 250 rule.

THE 250 RULE

I first read about the 250 rule in Joe Girard's best-selling book *How To Sell Anything to Anyone*. Girard is listed in the *Guinness Book of World Records* as the world's greatest salesman. He achieved this not through some extraordinary inbred skill but by a clear understanding of what makes people tick. He understands a great deal about human nature. His theory is simple: Everyone knows approximately 250 people well enough to invite them to a wedding or a funeral. They also know them well enough to tell them about you and your business, service, or product. Whatever it is you have to offer, each person you meet will talk about you. Not to 250 people at once, of course, but over the course of a year they will talk to friends at the local bar, at college, at work, or wherever they come into contact with them.

If what they have to say about you is good, when that group of 250 people talks to its own groups of 250 people a lot of folks are going to know what a wonderful person you are to meet and do business with. On the other hand, if everything that is said about you is bad—watch out! According to this principle, if you treat one person unfairly 250 people are going to find out. Whether you actually did treat that person unfairly does not matter, what matters is what they tell others.

PEOPLE ARE RIGHT NO MATTER
HOW WRONG THEY ARE

One of the simplest things you can learn about life is that when people feel they are right about something then they are right no matter how wrong they are. No amount of discussion or argument is going to change their mind, and even if it did they would hold a grudge against you forever.

When trying to get a different viewpoint across always leave your opponent a suitable line of retreat. It took me a lot longer than it should have to figure this out, but I have made far more friends by listening than by correcting.

GIVE WHEN YOU WANT TO GET!

When I first began writing books I wanted to get some PR for myself to promote a book that I had written about a particular industry. I sent out press releases to the six leading magazines in the industry. No one was interested, even though my book was the only how-to book in the industry designed to make a better living for everyone.

I followed my press release with a phone call to try and get the editors to run my story. I then discovered by accident the best way to get what you want from people: Give when you want to get. I should have known this principle all along but it took several instances of the principle in action before its full effect finally hit home.

While talking to one of the editors I happened to mention that I had found an excellent and profitable market for my books and I would like to write more, but simply did not have the time. Immediately his interest perked up. What kind of subjects did I want to tackle? Did I know that he had ghostwritten ten books and cowritten several others? Well, I didn't know these things but I was certainly willing to listen and we began building rapport.

The editor went on to tell me that he was not paid well so he frequently took on freelance work. Was I interested in him writing anything for me? I certainly was. Not only did he do an excellent job on the writing project but it also paid him well for his work. When I wrote a follow-up book I got fabulous PR in a major magazine. The idea worked so well that I tried it with a second magazine and then a third. Within a few weeks I had all three editors involved in writing projects with me. Since they were paid a commission based on sales, I had no out-of-pocket expenses and I wound up with my name, picture, and products splashed all over the country for free.

I have since used this principle on a weekly and often daily basis in one encounter or another. In fact, this very week I was negotiating a lease on a space in a major shopping center. The leasing agent met me in my office and asked me what type of terms I wanted from her and the center owner. Instead of laying down my terms right away I asked about the center's owner, whose decision is the final one on any lease. I asked how old he was, whether he played golf, and if he liked to work out.

She told me he was in his early forties, loved golf, and worked out at the gym several times a week. At the top of her sheet of paper I had her write my terms. First, I offered the owner a complimentary entry into my annual golf tournament. Second, I offered him and his family free karate lessons for as long as I rented the space in the center. Third, I offered him a copy of my book *Making it Big in America*. Being so successful, he obviously did not need it, but I told her I wanted to know whether he agreed with the main principles in it.

The agent wrote down all these things with a whimsical smile and stated that this was the most unusual lease proposal she had written in twenty years. I then concluded by asking for a 25 percent reduction in the asked for rent, six months free to start, and a full build out to my specs.

Within a few days I had a reply that granted almost all of my requests, this at a shopping center that would normally offer no such compromise due to its strong anchors and high volume of traffic.

Before you ask for the things you want consider first what it is that they want. What is the benefit to them if they help you in some way? Always look at any new encounter from the other person's perspective; to them it is the only one that matters. Show people first that you are willing to give and they will be more than happy to give back.

PEOPLE DON'T LIKE CRITICISM

The best way to get results in your dealings with others is by making positive not negative comments. Let me give you an example. I was hired as a consultant to watch classes at a karate school then provide suggestions to improve the instruction. The teacher was a young man of perhaps twenty-five. He was teaching a fifteen-year-old girl how to do a series of moves. During the ten minutes or so I watched the instructor I heard comments like this: "No! That's not how I showed you!" "Not like that. Like this." "What is the matter with you tonight?" "No, No, No!" The instructor was getting increasingly frustrated as was the girl. How do you think the girl felt at the end of class? Do you think she went home feeling great? Do you think she could hardly wait to come back the next night? This particular school was have trouble keeping its students involved in the program. Is there any wonder why?

In trying to get the most out of people no matter what you want them to do the key words are:

Good!
Great!
Excellent!
Well done!

When things are done wrong say:

Not quite
Better
Almost
Not bad, now let's make it perfect

Even those who ask you for criticism often don't want to hear anything negative. I was once in a meeting as a consultant when the CEO asked me for my opinion on the project at hand. I gave a fair and honest appraisal of how I saw it and recommended against the program. After the meeting the CEO shuffled me into a room and demanded to know what I thought I was doing. It turned out that this was his pet project.

It pays far greater dividends to find the positive qualities of people instead of their negative ones. As the old saying goes, you catch a lot more flies with honey than with vinegar.

Resolve to make at least three people feel good about themselves every day by complimenting them on something that you like about them, on their appearance, or on something they own. Resolve also to improve your communication skills and so enlist people to help you reach your goals.

LESSON 7

HOW TO
MARKET YOURSELF

If you want to succeed, people have to know that you exist and that you have something they want. Successful people know this so they make it a point to market themselves first before they market their product. There are two key aspects to marketing yourself: Knowing what people want (also known as knowing the market) and keeping yourself in front of them at all times. That's how you create the opportunity for new jobs, for promotions, and for business. It also makes it easier to succeed.

SUCCESS IS EASIER THAN FAILURE

It really is easier to make it big than to fail. This is because there is far less competition at the top than at the bottom. For example, for any given job opening only 5 percent of the people who apply actually stand any chance whatsoever of getting the job because 60 percent will be disqualified by a lack of qualifications or by a poorly written resume. That leaves just 40 percent to deal with, of which 10 percent will not hit it off with the interviewer; another 10 percent will not take the job if offered because their spouse won't want to move to another area or want their partner to take the job; 10% will turn it down because of kids, grandparents, or other family considerations; 3% will have some kind of black mark against them in their past like a reference that doesn't check out; and 2 percent will have some form of physical problem that will work against them with the interviewer, such as a nervous twitch or a heart condition. That leaves a slim 5 percent actually competing for the job.

KNOW YOUR MARKET

Of the five percent who make it to the final interview many will not be prepared for the interview. A friend of mine just applied for the city manager's job of a large city. He was one of twelve people who were included on the final short list for the position.

Wanting to make a good impression at the interview he flew into the city on Friday night, two days early. The following day he stopped at the local library, where he researched the city and its history. What he found there complemented the information he had already received by overnight mail from the chamber of commerce a few days earlier.

He spent Sunday driving around the town paying particular attention to the buildings, properties, parks, and operations run by the city. He made detailed notes on what he saw. He talked casually with the few city employees who were working on Sunday and asked them about their jobs, the city, the management, and their problems.

That evening he spent in his room reading the various local newspapers he had picked up during the day. They proved to be a great help in bringing to his attention the various issues that were on the forefront of people's minds in the area. He learned that a new garbage dump and a proposed prison were unpopular. The head of the school board was popular, having received national attention for his anti-drug program. A local community was holding a town meeting to discuss forming its own city.

At the interview the next day the committee thought he was surprisingly well informed and they subsequently called and offered him the job a few days later. In the short time that elapsed between his interview and their offer he was presented with another opportunity so turned the position down. But before he hung up he had a long discussion with the head of the interview panel.

The reason they had chosen him over several other higher profile applicants was because he was the only applicant who knew the first thing about the city or its problems. Several of the applicants did not even know the city's population or geographic size!

It's amazing, but twelve high caliber people applied for the same job and only one took the trouble to do any research. Yes, making it big really is easier than struggling along with the masses at the bottom.

The first rule of marketing is to know your market. Find out everything you can about your job, business, boss, customers, company, city, state and any other key information that may aid you in meeting their specific need. To do this often is as easy as going to your local library. Check *Who's Who* to find out about important people in your area. Check business registers to find out about executives and companies. Check with the local chambers of commerce to investigate a specific area and its history. If you lack knowledge about anything regarding the market for your talents or service, ask!

Boost Your Career Instantly

Try this on Monday morning for a quick boost to your career and a clear definition of your market area. Go into your boss's office and ask, "What could I do today to be more valuable to you? How could I improve my performance so that I can help the company reach its goals and objectives? How can I improve my value in the marketplace?" Once your boss has had time to get over the shock, listen very carefully to what he or she says. You have provided an opportunity for frank communication with you.

If you own your own business ask your customers point blank, "How could I make my services more valuable to you? What is it that you need or want? What will make you buy from me?"

If you are the boss try this in reverse to get your employees and subordinates behind you. Ask them how their working conditions could be improved so that they might become more effective and happier employees.

The Real Estate Agent's Lesson

A few years ago I was thinking about selling my home; the prices were rising rapidly in my area which would leave me with a tidy profit. On top of that I had a very interesting opportunity to purchase a beautiful piece property out of state. The deal on the new property had not yet been finalized so I decided simply to stick a for sale by owner sign on my house and see if there was any interest at the price I wanted.

Within two or three days of putting out the sign I was swamped with calls from local real estate agents. They left business cards, flyers, note pads, refrigerator magnets, and written notes. They all said basically the same thing: "Call me! I want to list your property!" Several followed up with phone calls that ranged from "Hi! I've never met you but I know we're going to be best friends" to a point blank "Let me have your listing. I'm the best."

They all told me they were the area's specialist and had sold more houses than anyone else that week, month, year, or decade depending on which period best suited their story. They all told me they were the top person in their office and a member of the million dollar club—whatever that is. They assured me that I did not need to speak to anyone else other than them.

Only one person of the twelve or so who pursued the listing showed any interest in my wants and needs. She actually took the trouble to put together a packet of information on my house and had it delivered it to my home. The packet was spiral bound and covered in card stock. On the front she had placed a label with my name typed in bold letters. Inside she listed the previous selling price, the tax rates, a detailed description of the property, and an overview of the area's schools, churches, shops, and services, clearly demonstrating to me that she knew all about the area in which she sold. She also included the selling prices of several similar homes in the area complete with pictures so I could compare them. She had a little graph establishing the price trends in the area and also included information on helping potential buyers get financing quickly. At the end of the package there was a warm, friendly letter and an invitation to call her if I decided to list the property with an agent.

Guess which agent I called.

As it happened I did not move, but I have recommended her to several people and I know she has received business from them. It cost her very little money to photocopy the few pages of information, information that was available to all the agents in the area. They all wanted me to help them make several thousand dollars by listing my home with them, but only one went to the trouble to help me. She marketed herself.

This is a perfect example of how poorly some so-called professionals market themselves, their products, and their services. Whatever it is you do, you must take the time and effort to present your case from the other person's side. You must know what they want, not just what you want. You must know your market!

NETWORKING

Networking was the big marketing word of the eighties and it still is important today. It is the technique by which successful professionals get most of their business. If I were to ask you to recommend an insurance agent or an accountant you could probably recommend someone for the job. That's networking. The key of course is to get your name on the tip of everyone's tongue ready to roll off when needed.

Develop a list of contacts in a wide variety of fields, not just your own. Keep every business card you are given instead of throwing them away. Write on the back of each card where and when you met the person and file each card under specific headings for future use. Invest in one of those large business card holders with plastic pockets so you can quickly find the one you need. Make it a point each week to drop a short note or to call five of the people in your card file. Create your own direct marketing force by getting to know as many people as possible and having them promote your business. If you have your own business and are in sales leave your business card everywhere you go: stick them on bulletin boards, put them on plates along with your tip at restaurants, hand them out to personnel at gas stations, hair salons, pizza stores—anywhere that makes sense for your product or service.

Join Business and Social Groups

Join local business groups such as the chamber of commerce, a breakfast club, or any such organization that consistently brings you into contact with potential employers, clients, and opportunities. Attend several trade shows and conventions each year in your industry and in other related industries. Attend meetings of hobby and special interest groups such as an auto club or model train group. Here you will bring yourself into contact with a large number of people with whom you already have a lot in common. If you are a little shy there is no better place to develop and increase your network than in such an easy and pleasurable environment. Networking is purely and simply a numbers game: The more people you know in your industry the greater your chances of advancing rapidly.

Keep Notes on Key People

Because of the sheer number of people you come into contact with, unless you are blessed with a photographic memory many people will quickly fade into the shadows of your mind. Ever received a phone call from Fred? You know, you pick up the phone and a voice is yelling enthusiastically "Hi! It's Fred!" Then there is the uncomfortable silence as your mind races to figure out who Fred is. The only Fred you can think of lives in Bedrock with his wife Wilma, his daughter Pebbles, and their pet dinosaur Dino.

In Harvey Mackay's book *Swim with the Sharks without Being Eaten Alive* he says that the one word of advice he would give to anyone trying to get ahead is "Rolodex." Mackay credits his success to the detailed personal questionnaire he has on all his friends, associates, and potential clients. Mackay's sixty-six questions detail the likes and interests of each individual. He jots the main points down on a Rolodex card for easy reference.

The power of this simple technique is amazing. I keep index cards on clients and friends in three small boxes on my desk. When are their birthdays? What are their hobbies? Where do they like to vacation? Where did they grow up? What type of activities are their children involved in? Their spouses? Over a period of time you will collect a wealth of personal information that will allow you develop and deepen rapport. This technique is especially important when you deal with a great number of people and you frequently must go several months before talking to them again.

Whenever a call comes in from a client or associate I have not spoken to in a while, my secretary tells me the name and I quickly flip through my index cards to refresh my memory of the person. As soon as I pick up the phone I start off by asking the caller an informed question based on my notes. This develops instant rapport and shows that I have taken the trouble to remember his or her interests. Recently, I picked up a software program called Ascend that has a great many features including an electronic phone book with lots of room for notes. I have begun putting all this information on computer, which will make it even more effective.

MARKET YOURSELF TO KEY PEOPLE

A big part of marketing yourself is simply keeping your name in front of key people so that when the time comes for them to act you will be the first one to get the call. That is why you probably have a note pad on your desk from your local real estate agent complete with his or her picture, company, and phone number. That's why AT&T, UPS, and a dozen other large companies send you calendars every year. It is why your top suppliers send you Christmas cards and maybe even a gift. It is also why every other pen, coffee mug, or glass in your business is adorned with a local bank's name, phone number, and logo. And let's not forget all those magnets at home on the refrigerator from the local doctor, dentist, gardener, and gas station. Everywhere you look people are vying to keep their name in front of you and the more creatively and successfully they mange to do it the more likely you are to use their products or services.

I get at least three birthday cards every year. One from my mother and father, one from my wife, and one from my insurance agent. He never misses and I think he must bribe the US Postal Service because, Sundays excepted, his card always shows up exactly on the right day. It costs him 32 cents plus a few cents extra for a generic card and it keeps him in my mind for referrals. It is always a simple thing but it works. Make it a point to find out the birthdays of key people in your life and put their names on a database. Send them a card on their birthday and at Christmas. You will be surprised over time what effect that will have on their thinking toward you.

Incidentally a person's birthday is an excellent day on which to approach them with an idea or to sell them on your products. Often when you pick up the phone and call someone through no fault of your own you catch them at a bad time or the person is in the middle of a bad day. The result is you do not get what you want out of the phone call. On a person's birthday, however, the people at home and at their office usually go out of their way to make the person feel special. This boosts their self-esteem and makes them far more receptive to ideas than they would be on any other day of the year.

Show Interest in Other People's Interests

Another great way to market yourself to key people is to send them items of interest to them. Newspaper or magazine articles on their business, industry, or hobby work well. Fax them reviews of pertinent books you think they might enjoy. Send notes with information on the comings and goings in their industry that might be of interest. Clip out the article of interest and add a simple note saying "I saw this and thought you would be interested. Best wishes." In short, keep in constant contact with key people and show them that you are interested in the things that they are interested in.

One easy way to do this is to subscribe to a clipping service. For a fee depending on the size of the area and the publications covered clipping services will send you all the articles run in local, state, and national media on any specific topic or person you wish to follow. This is a great way to look very smart with your boss and key contacts when you walk into the office with an article on your product or industry printed just days ago in a city three thousand miles away.

Don't Forget Spouses

If you are trying to develop a business relationship with a certain man make it a point to develop a cordial relationship with his wife or girlfriend. Many potential business relationships are wrecked at the start because of the indifferent attitude of a wife. I am sure this is also true in reverse. When introduced to the other half find out as much as you can about their interests and remember them. This information can be invaluable in developing a relationship. Win the favor of the spouse and you are more than halfway toward a good relationship with the other half.

This holds just as true for people who work for you as for people you are trying to impress. Your employees have wives and husbands who complain when they come home late or work weekends. That makes you the bad guy and it is not conducive to getting the most from people. The other half of the person's world can be an unseen thorn in your side. I have seen this happen too many times; however, there is a solution.

When rewarding an employee for good performance include the spouse in the event. Call home and ask where he would like to go for the weekend or what his favorite restaurant is. Then when you reward the employee for her work give the couple a weekend or a dinner at the place the husband suggested. The employee will be happy for the reward and the husband will be happy because he was asked and included. You are now the good guy.

MAKE FRIENDS AT BOTH ENDS OF THE LADDER

While it is important to spend as much time as possible with those at the top of the ladder of success, it is often very beneficial to befriend as many people as possible on the rungs below. Often these people hold the key to reaching the people above. Secretaries are, of course, a prime example: upset one and she can make reaching the person you want impossible. On the other hand, if you go out of your way to befriend her she can be an invaluable aid. Often people at the lower levels are in a position to push to get your ideas sent upstairs. The respect and consideration that you show them may be all they have ever received, so they are only to willing to help you further your goals. A simple thank you call or card to show your appreciation for their help will go a very long way toward securing it in the future.

KEEP YOUR FRIENDSHIPS IN REPAIR

Once you have gone to all the trouble to meet new people and become friends don't just collect their phone numbers and addresses. Do something with them. Here is an old-fashioned and underrated way to make a favorable impression on someone: Write them a letter. So few people take the trouble to do this these days with the phone, fax, and modem so close at hand, and yet that is the very reason it works so well. Can you remember a special letter from a friend? How did it made you feel knowing that they had taken the time to write? The very fact that you took the trouble to write a letter will get you remembered fast. As the well-known writer, Dr. Samuel Johnson said, "Keep your friendships in constant repair."

TAKE A CLIENT TO LUNCH

One way to stay in touch with people—clients, prospects, employees, or friends—is to take one to lunch each week. This can be a pleasurable and profitable way to keep relationships active. Lunching alone is a waste of valuable time.

Think of five people with whom you have almost lost touch. Write down their names and make it a point to call each this week and reestablish contact with them.

1. _____

2. _____

3. _____

4. _____

5. _____

LEARN HOW TO MAKE SPEECHES

As well as the many direct ways we have already discussed for marketing your talents there are also a couple of indirect ways that can help you reach a large number of people very quickly. The first of these is through public speaking.

There are few things in life that strike fear into the hearts of people more than the thought of having to speak in front of a large group. In a recent survey, fear of speaking in public was placed ahead of fear of dying. Now, that is an awfully stark statistic, yet public speaking offers a great way to market yourself. Speaking will allow you to both market your skills and meet new contacts. It demonstrates to others that you have knowledge in your field and it quickly positions you as an expert in that field provided, of course, that your presentation was good.

Although most people are desperately afraid of speaking, a few successes will quickly help them overcome their fears. The best way to start is to begin in front of a small group of friends or business associates. From there you build up to larger groups.

A key to effective speaking is to know your subject inside and out and to feel passionately about it. If you do not know your subject well others in your audience will quickly know and your speech will have little effect. If you know your subject well but do not feel passionately about it chances are your speech will come across with the same lack of interest that you feel.

Practice speaking on your own and record yourself on a cassette player. Study the speeches of famous orators and learn from their choice of words and delivery. There are many books and audio programs available both on the speeches of others and on how to improve your own technique or you can join a Toastmaster club, enroll at a local college for a night course in public speaking, or take a Dale Carnegie speaking course or some other such program. Your ability to communicate with others and to get your point across plays a huge part in your future success. Do not underestimate it.

What subjects do you know well enough to speak on, even if just for fifteen minutes?

1. _____
2. _____
3. _____
4. _____
5. _____

Where could you gain experience and exposure by speaking in your area? Perhaps the Elks Club, the Lions Club, or at a local charity? List five groups you could speak to.

1. _____
2. _____
3. _____
4. _____
5. _____

WRITING HELPS YOUR CAUSE

Writing is a great way to market yourself. Just like speaking, being in print positions you as an expert in your field. Start by writing short articles for your company newsletter or for local media and build up to trade and business publications. Once again, if you stick to those subjects you know well you will never go wrong. Keep copies of your published work to use later as backup material. If you can't get anyone to publish your work, publish it yourself.

When I founded my first advertising agency I desperately wanted to get some credibility and publicity for my agency. The first thing I did was to design and write a newsletter that would keep our potential clients informed of various subjects involved in making their advertising better. It was only four pages long and included articles on aspects of successful print advertising. I mailed out a thousand copies a month, covering the companies I wanted as clients. The first two issues received no response, but with the third issue I got a call and a new account. Each and every newsletter I sent out after the third one produced some kind of business for us.

Another small publication that I wrote was titled *How to Design an Ad That Works*. It was also a success. This simple publication was in the form of five pages of regular eight-and-a-half by eleven paper folded in half to form a twenty-page booklet. In it I described in very simple terms the basic principles of how to design a successful print ad. Not only did this booklet attract more work than anything else I ever did but it was also written up in local papers including the *Los Angeles Times,* which further helped the cause. As a point of interest, I sent it to the *Times* with a press release every year for four years before they ran the article on it—persistence pays off!

People Believe What They Read

People believe what they read—at least they believe more of what they read than of what they hear. Despite this age of skepticism there is a certain believability associated with things written in black and white. As a general rule people also believe that anyone who is published must possess some kind of special talent and be larger than life. Of course this is not true, but for our purposes, making you a success, don't tell anyone—just get something in print this year that lets people know you are an expert in something! I don't care if you collect garbage; you can still use writing to help you get ahead in life. (There is a lot interesting stuff in garbage to write about!) And if you feel you have absolutely no writing skills, jot down your ideas and have someone else help you. Call a friend, a local college student, or a professional service. It doesn't matter. Just get something in print! Make the effort to market yourself.

What area of your job or life do you know enough about to write an interesting or entertaining article?

What local publication could you submit an article to?

1. _____
2. _____
3. _____

Does your industry have a newsletter or trade magazine that you could submit an article to? List five possible publications below.

1. _____
2. _____
3. _____
4. _____
5. _____

Could you publish a simple booklet on job safety, cost cutting, stress relief, child rearing, self-defense, consulting, taxes, investments, real estate, selling, or any other subject that is related to your job or interests? Think hard. All you need is five or ten pages of simple but good information on any subject that other people might be interested in. List five subjects you could write about.

1. _____
2. _____
3. _____
4. _____
5. _____

How to Stand Out from the Crowd

Once you know your market thoroughly, have developed a list of contacts, and have promoted yourself it is time to go a step further. You must now work on standing out from the crowd.

A woman who attended one of my seminars recently submitted a resume for an accounting job. She delivered it in person and asked the secretary how many other people had applied. The secretary got up, walked to a tall four-drawer filing cabinet, and pulled open the first drawer: It was full of several hundred applications. She then pulled open a second drawer also full.

How can you get an interview, let alone a job, if you must compete with several hundred applicants—all of whom have similar resumes and qualifications? The answer is you must creatively market yourself in order to get noticed.

Most people who are job hunting make two key mistakes. First, they type out their resumes nice and neat and hope it matches all the others. But since the first obstacle to landing an interview is getting noticed, should they try to blend in with the crowd? No. Second, by submitting "generic" resumes job seekers ignore the fact that virtually every employer is looking for someone with creative problem-solving skills. If an applicant starts out by creatively solving the problem of how to get noticed, don't you think the prospective employer will be impressed?

Several years ago I applied for a job with an advertising agency. They ran an ad in a national publication seeking golf lovers to apply for a position with their agency. There was a huge response to the ad but they interviewed only a handful of people. Was I one of them? You bet your nine iron I was! I sent in my resume like everyone else, but unlike everyone else I typed it inside a picture of a large golf ball instead of on linen stationery. I got through two interviews before losing out to someone with a Madison Avenue background.

I have advised other people to approach resumes in this nontraditional way and they have also succeeded in getting initial interviews. While it may not work in some cases or in all industries, it does make your resume stand out from all the others in the file and greatly increases your chances of being called—especially if the people making the decision admire creativity or are visually oriented. Even if they are not, your resume will be one of the few, perhaps the only one, remembered at the end of the day.

Let's get back to the woman I mentioned who was seeking the accounting job. Instead of a traditional resume she could have placed her resume inside a picture of a calculator with a headline like "Ann Smith: Creative Solutions to Your Company's Accounting Problems." A computer salesperson could use a large graphic of a computer with the resume printed on the screen. You can get background graphics like these from any graphics business and at almost every print shop.

The Audio Approach

Another interesting way to stand out is to include an audio tape along with your written resume. Place a bright-colored label with the words "PLAY ME" in bold letters on the cassette. It's just like in *Alice's Adventures in Wonderland* where she comes across a bottle labeled "Drink Me." What does she do? She drinks it of course! Most people can't resist when confronted with this approach. In your cover letter ask the interviewer to play the tape on the way from work that evening. Mention that the tape is only a few short minutes long and that you think it will save him or her a lot of time and hassle with the interviewing process if they listen.

Start off the tape by thanking the listener for taking valuable time to listen to you. Then quickly and concisely tell the listener exactly how you will help the company if you are chosen. You might point out that you customarily go to great lengths to ensure that a job is done well. Sending the tape will reinforce this fact in the listener's mind.

If you work in a more conservative industry where you feel this might be a little risky try making up a brochure on yourself. Take an eight-and-a-half by eleven piece of paper and fold it twice, forming three panels. Put your name, address, and phone number on the far right panel. If your looks are an asset include your photograph. On the center panel place your resume in brief. Head the panel "Resume Highlights." On the far left panel complete a number of one- or two-line sentences that describe why the company should hire you. Head this panel "The Benefits of Hiring John Smith." For example:

- With more than three years of industry-specific selling experience John Smith is ready to represent your products.

- John Smith is self-motivated, so you know he will always give you his best.

On the inside panel list one or two key headlines such as experience, product knowledge, and enthusiasm. Underneath each write a few sentences on how these qualities you possess will help the company. By presenting your resume like this you are showing that you have some marketing skills, creative skills, and problem solving skills. This will almost always work in your favor when it comes time to getting an interview.

There is really no end to the creative ways you can increase your chances of landing a better job and better pay. In Los Angeles, one young actress who couldn't seem to get a break spent every dime she had renting a giant billboard on Sunset Boulevard in Hollywood. On it she put her picture and a plea for work. Within days the investment in the billboard was repaid in the form of a movie role.

Marketing yourself to others is a process you must continue do even after your short-term goals are reached.

You must keep yourself on the mind of others so they can open up potential opportunities for you, both now and in the future.

Five Ways I Will Improve the Way I Market Myself or My Business

1. _____
2. _____
3. _____
4. _____
5. _____

Resolve now to constantly market yourself to stand out from the crowd.

LESSON 8

HOW TO SELL YOURSELF

L ike it or not your success or failure in life will ultimately depend a great deal on your ability to sell. Whether you make your living selling tangible products like computers or cars, as millions of American do, or you spend you career stuffed behind a desk with no public contact, selling yourself is of vital importance. Even if you never sell a tangible product your entire life you are still involved in sales every day you are alive.

You have to sell someone on your unique abilities in order to get hired. You have to sell your worth and talents to your boss in order to move up the corporate ladder or to get a raise. You have to sell yourself to your customers, your staff, and even your friends. You have to sell yourself in order to get accepted into a university, get engaged, or take out a new car loan. Almost every action in life revolves around some sort of selling.

THE IMPORTANCE OF A WINNING ATTITUDE

The first law of selling yourself to others is to develop a winning attitude. Success depends not only on your

attitude toward others but also on your attitude toward
yourself. How is your attitude: Is it positive, optimistic,
and happy? Or is it negative, pessimistic, and destructive
to success?

The Welder's Lesson

Have you ever noticed how three people can view the same
situation with totally different attitudes and usually with
totally different results? Many years ago a small boy stood
at the edge of San Francisco Bay. From the banks of the
beautiful bay he looked down at an army of men and ma-
chines. He was naturally inquisitive, as small boys often
are, and slowly wandered down to a group of three men
welding a series of huge metal girders. When he reached
the first he ask him what he was doing. The man gruffly
replied that he was working for his lousy paycheck. The
boy walked over to the second man and asked the same
question. He replied in a gentler tone, but with an equal
lack of enthusiasm, that he was welding together some
pieces of metal. When he reached the third worker the
man looked up and smiled happily at the young boy. The
boy asked him the same question. The man replied, "I'm
building the greatest bridge the world has ever seen!" The
boy's face lit up in wonder and he went on his way.

Here were three men from similar backgrounds with
identical jobs, each working under the same conditions,
with the same hours, and for the same pay, yet each held
a totally different attitude toward his work. You have seen
examples of this in your life. Based on your experience,
which man was most likely to succeed?

I have never met anyone with a "nine-to-five attitude"
who has been successful. What is a nine-to-five attitude?
It's the attitude held by the type of people who come in at
9:00 A.M. on the dot and then spend fifteen minutes getting
ready to work. Their lunch hours are an hour and fifteen

minutes and they take several coffee breaks during the day. At a quarter to five all work stops and at five the only burst of speed and enthusiasm seen that day is used to get them out the door. People with this attitude complain about having to work late once a month and always feel that the boss is exploiting them. They are the type of people who think that life owes them an existence and that the person who exerts the least amount of effort wins.

This type of attitude is as prevalent in unsuccessful people as it is lacking in those who reach the top. Possessing a good attitude has a great deal to do with success. Successful people look for ways to get more work done in less time because they know that this will pay off in the long run. Successful people know they must give more if they want to get more.

DEVELOP A WINNING ATTITUDE

Attitudes are generally formed when we are young and model those of our parents. This is great if your parents had a good attitude but not so great if they did not. For example, if your parents held attitudes that were prejudicial toward one group of people, then chances are you at least started out with the same type of attitude. Over time you might have met someone from that group who did you a good turn and became your friend, thus changing your attitude. But you also might have had such a poor attitude toward this group that you never let yourself meet anyone who could change your attitude.

Attitudes are formed in three ways: They come from our beliefs or knowledge, from our feelings and emotions, or from our tendencies to act in a specific way based on knowledge and emotion.

If you realize that you have a poor attitude toward people or work then you need to address your attitude and make some adjustments. Otherwise selling yourself will be impossible. Have you ever wondered why so many Korean, Vietnamese, and other Asian immigrant families who came to this country with nothing are so successful? It is because the Asian culture has a built-in attitude to hard work. They come to this country and work extremely hard. It is no surprise they get ahead faster than many people who were born here.

The first step in making sure your attitudes are consistent with those of successful people is to make a quick and honest review of them. Ask yourself:

Do I have a good attitude toward myself?

Do I have a good attitude toward my work?

Do I have a good attitude toward those I work with?

Do I have a good attitude toward my boss?

Do I have a good attitude toward people in general regardless of color or creed?

Do I have a good attitude toward life and the rewards it holds for me?

If you answered any of these questions "No" examine this attitude further and ask yourself why you have this attitude. What caused you to think this way even if you know that it is counterproductive?

Once you have isolated the reason you can set about changing it. If, for example, you discover that you have a poor attitude toward work because you were passed over for a promotion you can now look for ways to change your attitude. Here are some suggestions. You can:

1. Change companies and start with a clean slate.

2. Put in extra effort so that you get the next promotion.

3. Leave and enter an entirely new field.

4. Continue your poor attitude and make life unpleasant for everybody. You can ruin your previous good

conduct record and perhaps even get yourself fired in the process.

Now, which sounds better to you? Whichever option you choose, only one guarantees failure. The others all offer opportunity.

Expect the Best

Expecting the best, or maintaining an attitude of positive optimism, is another key ingredient in the recipe for success. Successful people are by nature positive people; they expect things to work out for the best. They see the half-empty glass as half full. They take setbacks in stride and see them not as insurmountable obstacles but as stepping stones toward success.

Successful people expect to reach their goals. They expect to have fun and lead a happy life. Successful people remove the words "can't" and "if" from their vocabulary. They replace them with "can" and "when." To them "if I become rich" becomes "when I become rich."

By maintaining this type of positive mental outlook, their subconscious mind does all that it can to help them reach their goals. Remember, the mind will only do what you ask it to do.

Focus on the things that go right in your life, not on the things that go wrong. Take small successes and accomplishments and tell yourself what a good job you did to achieve these minor successes. In order to achieve success you must be able to see yourself as a successful person. If you have trouble with self-confidence or self-esteem I highly recommend that you enroll in a good martial arts program.

Martial arts programs improve your physical and mental fitness. Good programs are designed to reward you with different colored belts at regular intervals to display your achievement of goals, thus proving to you that you have what it takes to become successful. This excellent system of rewards is one of the reasons martial arts have become so popular in this country. By the way, forget the old notion that martial arts are violent and are just for macho men. The martial arts are designed for men, women, and children of all ages, from five to seventy and beyond. Taking a course is one of the best investments you can make in yourself because it builds a positive attitude.

Attitude is Everything

I believe that my attitude is what helped me become successful so quickly. Although my story may sound like a rags to riches story it really is not. I was brought up in a good home and at eighteen simply decided to come to America. The few hundred dollars I brought with me ran out quickly and there were many times over the next two years when my net worth amounted to my golf clubs and a small bag of clothes. I frequently slept in my car and lived from day to day, but I never once felt poor. You see, you are only broke when your mind has lost its dreams and your body is too tired to look for them. I never felt the world was against me or that anyone owed me a break.

I always felt like a millionaire and because I felt like a million dollars I often hung out and played golf with real millionaires who had no idea that I did not have a dollar to my name. I joined them as their guest at polo games and even at their parties where I met even more interesting people.

I never once even considered going back to England even though it would have meant comfort and security. I toughed it out simply because life did not seem that difficult, and armed with the attitude that success was a foregone conclusion I knew it was just a matter of time before things would work out they way I wanted them to. Having a good attitude makes the next step in selling yourself much easier to accomplish.

The Secret of Selling Yourself

Do you know how to sell people on you, your products, or service and then keep them buying forever? It is incredibly simple, nevertheless most people will not bother to take the small amount of extra effort necessary to do it. Will you? It doesn't matter if you work as a waiter or own a chain of twenty stores; this simple idea works. It worked two hundred years ago, it works today, and it will work two hundred years from now. Are you ready for the revelation?

Always do a little more than you are paid for. That's right, not a little less, a little more. Instead of leaving at a quarter to five, stay until a quarter after. Always give a little more service than people expect. Give 101 percent at work or don't waste your time at work at all. Take the rest of the day off. By always going the extra mile you instantly vault yourself over 95 percent of the other people in your line of work. So few people put in anything close to 100 percent effort that by putting in 101 percent you are not working just 1 percent harder than the rest but more like 40 or 50 percent harder. This extra effort will compound at an astonishing rate and allow you to progress more rapidly than you can imagine.

Ask yourself honestly, "Do I give 101 percent to every aspect of my job or business?" Unless I miss my guess, the answer is no. You may give 101 percent sometimes. You may give 101 percent when you like your boss or a particular project, but what about when you don't? I frequently talk with people at the golf club who tell me with glee that their company thinks they are making a sales call or attending a meeting. That is not giving 101 percent and over time their careers will stagnate.

Santos' Lesson

A few years ago I put an ad on a bulletin board at the little store near my home. I was looking for someone to work part-time at my home office to help me finish projects on the weekends and in the evenings. The job required someone with typesetting and computer skills.

As I worked late one night my dogs began to bark furiously and there came a knock at the door. I opened it and there stood a young man neatly dressed in brown corduroy pants and a golf shirt. In broken English he introduced himself as Santos and explained that he had seen my advertisement for a typesetter.

He had almost no experience and spoke very poor English, yet there was something about him I liked. He was working at a nearby stable looking after horses and getting paid less than minimum wage for sixty hours of work. He told me right off that there would be no charge for his services until I was completely satisfied with the quality of his work—no matter how long it took. Well, an offer like that is hard to refuse! I gave him a small project and he left. He returned a few days later with the job I had given him. It was full of typos and spelling mistakes but he told me he had just enrolled in night classes at the local junior college to improve both his PageMaker skills and his English.

Over the next few weeks his skill improved dramatically but it was still not good enough to use for my important projects. Then several months went by before I saw him again. He told me he had been to Mexico. While there he had continued his studies and bought a Spanish version of the software instruction manual. He was now doing a good job. I started using him and paying him at once. The same week he was let go at the stables in favor of someone who would work for even less money than he was making. I made Santos a full-time employee.

He spent most of his paycheck on new computer programs, hardware, and courses that furthered his skills.

Just four months later he was designing a new mail order program for my business. Now when I go to the office late in the evening or on weekends he is often there. Santos is a perfect example of how to sell yourself and get ahead in life. Despite having poor language skills and working long hours for just enough money to eat, he turned his situation around in just over twelve months. He is now a valuable employee and although I wish his English were a little clearer, it has never held him back from investing in himself, taking action, and selling himself. He has gone from a dead end job to an exciting position in a company that offers an excellent future.

Recently he asked if his wife could join my staff. Despite his fast rise in my organization and a big change in his lifestyle he offered the same terms for his wife to start as he did for himself: "She works for nothing until you are happy with her work." The offer was not necessary, her work was already well-deserving of pay.

My Own Examples

In order to sell yourself you often have to work for nothing. When I first came to the United States I worked at the Wellington Golf Club in West Palm Beach, Florida, for over nine months with no pay, on the understanding that I could play free golf. During this time I survived by playing golf with an old man named Pat Macarry. Every night we bet five dollars. Occasionally he won, but more often than not I could count on winning twenty-five dollars a week. He was really just helping me out in a way that made us both feel good about it.

Despite my lack of money, the time I spent at the golf club was extremely valuable. The people I met and the relationships I developed had a huge influence on the next ten years of my life. At the time I walked into their pro shop, they did not have an opening, but they hired me because I offered to work for free. Later on I did get put on the payroll and that laid the foundation for a successful life.

In effect both Santos and I came with money-back guarantees. We were working for nothing and so the risks were low. It was simply up to us to sell ourselves enough to others to turn that start into a paying job.

When I lived in Florida during the time I was in college I also worked in a restaurant in Lake Worth. They had a staff of over thirty people and on any given day five or six people did not show up for work. Some would call in sick, others just did not show and spent the day at the beach instead. It was unbelievable to me. In the three years I worked as a waiter or at the golf club I never called in sick or missed a day of work. Sure I sometimes got sick but I might just as well work with a cold as lie in bed and do nothing. I also never showed up late. It wasn't that I loved my job, but I truly believed that if you are at work you should give it your all or go do something else.

During my first few days at the restaurant I had some type of disagreement with the manager, I can't even remember what it was about, but the following week he took me off the schedule. In short, I was fired. I came in to work the lunch shift and saw my name was not on the schedule. I went to see the assistant manger and asked what was going on. He told me that for some reason the manager had decided to let me go. Of course I asked why, but he didn't know. I did not want to be fired since I was in college and needed the income to support myself and to save enough money so I could spend the summer in Europe. As it was getting close to the end of the season, finding another job quickly would have been a pain, so I decided to be un-fired.

Instead of leaving, I asked where he wanted me to work that day and pointed out that it was almost time to open. He looked at me and then looked at his watch. He also noticed that no one else had yet shown up although

we were indeed just minutes from opening for business.
He then assigned me an area of tables to wait on. The
next day I showed up again despite not being on the
schedule. This went on for a week before I walked in and
the manager who had fired me was there. He looked at
me and asked the assistant manger if he had put me
back on the schedule. He said no, that I was the only
waiter who he could ever count on to show up on time
everyday and who never called in sick. The manger
looked at me hard for a minute and said then said,
"Okay, I will put you back on the schedule." After that we
became good friends and I also wound up making what I
thought at the time was a great deal of money for a
young college student.

Here is another example. One morning about seven
o'clock I went out to my car, a '65 Ford Mustang in two-
tone—silver and rust. It was a real classic, at least that's
what they told me when I bought it. The problem that
morning was it wouldn't start. I was due at the golf club
by 7:30 and I had to drive over seven miles to get there. At
that point I could have called and told them that I could
not make it in, after all I had a good excuse. Instead, I
started to run toward the club. After running about four
miles as fast as I could one of the members on his way to
the course recognized me and gave me a ride the rest of
the way. I arrived at 7:29.

At the time I thought nothing of this extra effort. I
had a job, so what if it only paid $3.75 an hour. I had made
a commitment to be there and I was going to keep it at all
costs. It was only after years of dealing with others, including my own employees, that I realized how unusual
this simple act of effort was. I am convinced that no matter what your age or background giving a little extra effort
will pay off big and do so quickly. The reason is simple; so
few people give anything near their best effort that it is remarkably easy for you to shine no matter what business or
industry you are in.

Avoid the Curse of Being Average

Actor Woody Allen says, "Ninety percent of the job is just showing up." That's true up to a point but it's not enough for you to get ahead. It just puts you in the average category.

In the course of my travels around the country as a consultant I come into contact with a great many people from all kinds of backgrounds—from corporate executives to high school seniors hoping to get into college. I've rarely met someone who gives 101 percent.

I listen to people's comments and complaints about their jobs and their bosses. I seldom hear people talking about ways they could help their company grow or ways they could increase productivity. Instead, they talk about poor benefits, impatient supervisors, and other negatives. Have you ever seen one of those interviews on television where people just out of work tell the reporter that no one wants to give them a job? Somehow they believe the world owes them a living. They are in for a harsh dose of reality-based shock therapy.

To quote the well-known words of John F. Kennedy, "Ask not what your country can do for you; ask what you can do for your country?" Get used to asking yourself how you can do more in your present job or business to improve your value to your boss and your customers. The more you do for them the more they will do for you in the form of promotions and sales. Hard work always pays off, although it does not always pay off instantly or as quickly as you would like. Nor does it always pay off in the way you though it would, but in the end it does pay off.

List ten specific areas where you can increase your effort at work or in your personal life up to 101 percent. For example, show up on time every day, waste less time, call one extra prospect each day.

1. _____
2. _____
3. _____
4. _____
5. _____
6. _____
7. _____
8. _____
9. _____
10. _____

Now list five positive things that may result over the next few months due to this extra effort. Perhaps you will receive extra business, a promotion, or a raise.

1. _____
2. _____
3. _____
4. _____
5. _____

KNOW YOUR PRODUCT

The second law of selling is to have confidence and faith in your product and in yourself, which in many cases is the product. Become an expert in your product and how your product offers solutions to people's problems. All too often you run across people who know nothing about their product.

Recently I was with a friend who was looking to buy a new car. Usually he drove German sports cars but on this occasion he had read a very positive article on the latest Corvette and he decided to go and see one. Once in the showroom a young, well-dressed salesman approached and introduced himself to us. My friend started to ask questions about the car like, "How much more horsepower does it have compared to the previous model?" and "How has it changed from the earlier version?" The salesman could not answer even one of my friend's questions. Instead he hemmed and hawed before eventually announcing that he usually sold Chevettes not Corvettes. He then scurried off to look for another salesman.

The second man was far more polished and professional. He knew a great deal about Corvettes, but even he could not tell us what had changed between this model and the previous one, except to assure us that this one was indeed better. How it was better? Why it was $5,000 more? He couldn't tell us.

Both of these salesmen could have found out about their product by simply reading the glossy brochures in the racks or by picking up a copy of *Road & Track* magazine, but neither did. My friend in fact knew a great deal more about the product than they did.

Needless to say we left and he bought a car elsewhere. He bought a Lotus Esprit from a man who knew the car inside out. This salesman actually spent his own money and vacation time to travel to England and visit the factory where they were made. He was a member of the Lotus Owners' Club and was passionate about his product.

It is essential that you know everything that you can about what you sell and exactly how each feature can benefit your customer. You must be able to take objections and turn them into sales. This is just as true for selling yourself as it is for selling a tangible product. Push your strong points and don't dwell on your weak points.

Recently an acquaintance of mine, an executive who is fifty-five years old, told me it was impossible for him to get another job because employers thought that he was too old. I told him that as long as he agreed with that line of thinking he was certainly not going to get very far. He said that he didn't feel that way but that he couldn't come up with a counter to their objections.

I advised him to discuss his age right up front and make that his main selling point. During the 1984 presidential campaign Ronald Reagan's age, seventy-six, became a factor in the press and was brought up again during the first debate. During the second debate when the question was asked again, Reagan skillfully turned the question around by saying, "I will not make age an issue in this campaign. I am not going to exploit for political purposes my opponent's youth and inexperience." Everyone, including Walter Mondale, laughed and the issue of age never came up again. For many people, Reagan's entire campaign swung into gear on these few lines and as a result he never looked back.

Design an Ad Featuring You

Here is an interesting and entertaining way to bring your particular attributes to the surface. Imagine that you are the head of a large advertising agency and you have been hired to design a national advertising campaign to run in all the major newspapers and magazines. The product you have to sell is you.

Take a sheet of paper and on the very top paste a picture of yourself. Make sure it is a good picture because this is an important campaign. Under the picture write your name along with the words *can help your business dramatically!* You now have an attractive picture and a headline that no company can resist. (If you own your own business think up a headline that promises something to your customer.)

Now comes the creative part. Under your headline you must explain in the space that is left why you can dramatically improve this company's business. This will force you to think of which of your skills are most valuable and how you can portray this to others. For example, explain how your thirty years of experience will save the company from costly mistakes, how your extensive network of buyers and contacts will increase business quickly, and how your stable family life makes you a better manager.

If you are young stress your enthusiasm, your energy, your ability to work long hours, your team spirit, and your thirst for knowledge. Your ad should contain at least five reasons why you are a great choice. Keep your ad in a safe place and refer to it periodically so you can add to it and redesign it as you increase in knowledge and ability.

Package Yourself Attractively

Packaging is the third key ingredient in selling. While attitude and knowledge are important, if the total package isn't pleasant your prospective customer will pass. We all know that first impressions are the key to establishing a relationship. If you can't get to first base, you will never score a home run. People form first impressions quickly based on the initial image you present to them. It is a fact that how you package a product directly influences the public's acceptance of it. Imagine going into a supermarket for a box of breakfast cereal and seeing cartons that are dirty, crushed, or torn. Would you purchase one? Of course not; you would look for a clean undamaged carton even though the cereal inside the damaged box might well be just as good as that in the undamaged box.

When you intend to meet new people, think about exactly what "package" you need to present to appeal to them. This package concept isn't concerned solely with the outside, but take into account character qualities as well. What is the total picture you want to present? Think of yourself as if you were up on a supermarket shelf along-side a dozen other executives or business owners. Would shoppers choose you?

Have you ever noticed that fancy restaurants or ex-clusive hotels only park the real nice cars up front by the entrance. It's always the Porsches, Ferraris, Rolls Royces, Mercedes, and Lincolns that get the best spots. The rest of the cars are relegated to the back lot. As a car drives up the valets decide how this car and the person in it will be treated before it even rolls to a stop. It is much the same with your personal appearance and attitude. You may not be able to afford a Rolls Royce but you can make yourself look like a success without much trouble at all.

Dress Appropriately

While there is little you can do to change your physical ap-pearance short of radical surgery, there is a great deal you can do with the your personal appearance in terms of shoes, clothes, and accessories. A large part of selling your-self is looking good; America is rightly or wrongly a very visual society. While at times you might think how great it would be to dress in blue jeans and grow your hair long like a rock star, success frequently demands something different.

Your initial reaction to anyone you meet is almost al-ways based on looks. For example, suppose you were sit-ting in an outdoor cafe and a guy walked up to you looking like he slept in his clothes. What would your first reaction be? Most likely it wouldn't be one of bonding. In fact you would probably go out of your way to avoid contact.

Are you dressed right now like the successful person you want to be? Are your clothes pressed and your shoes shined? Is your hair combed? Go out of your way to im-prove your appearance. Buy a couple of new suits that fit the image of the successful person you are or intend to become. Throw away the plastic sports watch and get a nice looking dress watch. Review your wardrobe at least once a year so that you are not left in the dark ages in terms of changing fashion. One sure sign that a person is getting "old" is that they stop buying clothes. Have you ever noticed how most senior citizens wear the styles and colors of twenty years ago? They look and move like old people because they think like old people. It's seldom because they can't afford new clothes; it's simply that they don't care any more. Then you have a person like former President Reagan who even though he is in his eighties still has great looking suits and vibrantly enjoys life. It's because he still cares. When you stop caring about little things you stop caring about bigger things as well.

List five ways you can upgrade your personal appearance no matter how good you look now. For example, do you need a new watch, suit, or haircut?

1. _____
2. _____
3. _____
4. _____
5. _____

Display Winning Body Language

It's amazing the degree to which people react to you based on little things like your smile. When you are introduced to people, always greet them with a warm and friendly smile. Shake their hand firmly and confidently; there are few things that turn off people quicker than a limp handshake. If you stand up straight, pull your shoulders back, put your chest forward, and make good eye contact you tell the other person by your body language that you are indeed glad to meet them and that you are a successful and confident individual.

Mind Your Manners

Another one of those little things that is often overlooked is manners. If you listen to many older people talk you'll hear them say how people today seem to have no manners. And, you know, maybe they have a point. While I can't claim that I don't occasionally scoop peas onto my fork or put my elbows on the dinner table I do make it a strong point to at least say "Thank you" to everyone at appropriate times. I hold doors open for people, help them pick things up when they drop them, and generally try to show good manners at all times. I do this with everyone, waiters, gas station attendants, store clerks, and absolutely everyone I come into contact with who does anything for me. It costs nothing to be polite, and over time it is noticed and applauded by others. Make it a point to start being polite to everyone you encounter. "Please" and "Thank you" go a long way when you're trying to build a good image.

As we draw closer to a global economy more businesses find that they must do business overseas. Attention to manners and customs is especially important when dealing with a foreign country because it can critically influence your acceptance and ultimate success. Many countries like Japan or Saudi Arabia have customs that are completely different from our own. Pick up a small guidebook on the country you are dealing with. It will give you a head start in learning local customs. You can also make a favorable impression by applying what you have read when you meet a foreigner visiting this country. Once again it is a simple case of showing a little extra effort— effort that will always pay off handsomely.

Don't Forget to Follow Up

The final part of selling is following up. If you are selling a product the sale does not end when your clients have signed on the dotted line. Continue the relationship you have worked so hard to cultivate by providing the kind of service that keeps your clients coming back and recommending you to their friends. Likewise, if you are selling yourself, the selling process does not stop with getting hired or getting the next raise or promotion. Throughout your career you will be selling yourself to others until you make it all the way to the top, and even then you must continue to sell to shareholders, directors, and your co-workers. Make the extra effort to sell yourself every day.

Resolve to maintain a good attitude, to package yourself attractively, and to continue selling yourself every day.

LESSON 9

HOW TO SOLVE YOUR PROBLEMS

FACING THE PROBLEMS OF LIFE

If you want to live your dreams don't let problems get in your way—you just can't. In order to make it big you must face countless roadblocks and obstacles on your path to the top, all of which must be circumvented in order to reach your goals. It is at this stage, even armed with goals, strategies, and a plan, that most people become derailed. Isn't it easier to jump out of bed every morning and rush to work when things are going well? It is not so easy when faced with the daily problems of life.

Handling problems is just like handling objections in a selling situation in that once they are solved they become stepping stones to success rather than obstacles. To put it another way, think of each problem you encounter in life as a gate on the road to the top. Once you have figured out how to open the gate you will be that much closer to achieving your goals. Unfortunately, once the majority of people find that the gate is locked and that they do not have the key to open the lock right there in their pocket they simply turn around and go home.

The people who make it big in life never let the fact that they don't have a key to the gate hold them back. They try to pick the lock or climb over the gate. They try to squeeze under it or through it. They may try to break it down or, when all else fails, they try circumventing the gate by finding another route that takes them where they want to go. Often the knowledge they gain from solving such problems or the fact that they are forced to choose another route actually speeds up their progress rather than hindering it.

The key to solving your problems is to step out of your conventional wisdom and become creative. People who fail to make it big look at a problem, let's say a lack of capital, and say, "I can't do this until I have more money." At this point they stop thinking and their mind shuts down. It shuts down simply because that is what it has been instructed to do. An urgent message is sent to the brain that says "Don't think about this problem again until we get more money and can proceed." The brain says, "Fine" and shuts down.

It shuts down despite the fact that the lack of a creative solution may mean getting a second job and working overtime for months to save the money. But this will never be the answer because people who handle problems in this way are always one problem away from starting their journey to the top. Even if they solve their present problem by saving for six more months, another problem will arise and they will be stumped again.

People who are successful and are lacking capital look at the problem and ask, "How can I get this money? What if I try this or maybe that to raise it?" They begin studying the problem instead of simply looking at it and hoping that it will somehow disappear. When faced with any problem it is important to analyze it to make sure it doesn't get any bigger.

THREE STEPS TO EFFECTIVE PROBLEM SOLVING

There are three simple but crucial steps to problem solving that must be employed if you are serious about solving problems on a regular basis, and let me assure you that in order to be truly successful you must solve your problems.

Step One: Identify the Problem to be Solved and Write It Down in Detail

The first step in problem solving is to clearly identify the problem. Exactly what problem are you going to solve? Or, more basically, what is a problem? That in itself is an interesting question. What poses a problem to one person is another person's opportunity or routine action. For example, imagine you are in a small plane with two friends returning from a fishing trip. Suddenly the pilot has a heart attack and becomes unconscious. Is this a problem? It certainly is for the sick man but not necessarily for you. You might be able to fly a plane on your own or the third man may be an airline pilot. In this case one of you would simply take over the controls and land the plane. If you are a doctor your problems may be gone completely. You might recognize that the victim had a mild heart attack and is now breathing normally and so the imminent danger is over. If, of course, you are not a doctor and no one else can fly the plane you have a problem—a big problem. But do you see what I mean? That which often appears as an insurmountable problem to one person can simply disappear when seen through the eyes of another.

Now this may sound funny, but many people set out to solve a problem and in their enthusiasm they solve the wrong problem. As a result they leave the initial problem untouched, still operating in their lives. They find that they have wasted time solving problems that weren't the real problems. Famous band leader Count Basie was upset because the piano on which he played was constantly out of tune. He told the club owner that he would not return to his club again until the piano was fixed. A few days later the owner called to say that everything was all right. When Basie returned he was furious when he found that the piano was still hopelessly out of tune. "I thought you fixed this?" he yelled at the owner. "I did," protested the stunned owner. "I had it painted. There is not a single scratch on it!"

Another interesting example of clearly defining the actual problem happened in an up-scale apartment building in New York. The exclusive apartment building had only one set of elevators and there were growing complaints from the tenants about the amount of time it took to get up and down in the building. Several engineers, consultants, and elevator specialists were called in to study the problem. Many solutions were suggested. Unfortunately most dealt with adding more elevators, which was not feasible in the old building. Another solution focused on trying to speed up the existing elevators with computer controlled smart programming of the elevators, but even this would not bring the speed up significantly.

One of the tenants who worked in the fashion business heard about the attempts to solve the problem and put forward one of her own. Instead of proposing a solution that involved messing around with the elevators, she suggested adding mirrors around the elevator waiting area! She felt that the real problem wasn't the time it took for the elevator to travel up or down, rather it was that people used the time to think about how much time was being wasted waiting for the elevator. Taking a basic principle of human nature "people love to talk about themselves" she reasoned that they also loved to look at themselves and the real problem was solved. Now people stand patiently in the lobby waiting for the elevator, all the while checking themselves out in the mirror. Because they have something interesting to do to pass the time they actually think that the elevators have speeded up.

Take a piece of paper and clearly define your problem listing its individual components. For example, let's suppose you wrote, "My business is not profitable." This is your problem statement. Now list all the components of the problem. Your business is not profitable because (1) sales are down, (2) your product is faulty, (3) your accounting system doesn't track your expenditures. You must clearly define the problem if you expect to solve it.

It is important to note that many problems are very complex and thus need to be broken down into a series of smaller component problems. The trouble in solving most everyday problems is that they are often poorly defined. The actual problem runs into another problem and the desired outcome seems hazy at best. For example, suppose you believe that the lack of profitability of your business is due to a lack of money coming in. That is a vague problem that must be further defined into a specific amount, say you need to take in at least $5,000 a month. This gives you a clear definition of the problem and a clear goal. Now let's try to solve that problem.

Identifying the problem clearly will ensure that you face the problem with the clarity necessary to solve it. A problem that is extremely complex and has multiple facets will be a source of frustration because the problem is too large to tackle all in one effort. Breaking the problem down to a smaller, more manageable size will help you solve the problem.

Step Two: List the Constraints

Once you have written down the problem, the next step is to list all the constraining factors that you believe are connected with the problem. In the example above, one of the constraints might be that you cannot afford a new accountant or that you are short on staff. Since you believe this is a problem you should identify it as a believed constraint. List all such constraints and carefully analyze them to ensure they are real constraints. Often when you take yourself through this part of the problem-solving process and look carefully at each constraint you will expose false beliefs that can be removed revealing quick and easy solutions.

In my karate studio people frequently test to advance to the next rank. I devised a simple problem few students—from young children to adult executives—have been able to solve. During the student's examination I hold a long wooden staff called a *bo* in my hand. It is six feet long and about two or three inches in circumference. At the end of the test I take each student and hand him or her the staff. I give these simple instructions: "Use this staff to keep your feet off the ground for ten seconds."

I hand the staff to the student vertically. Invariably the student—whether young or old—cheerfully plants the thin pole in the carpet and tries to climb it and balance on it like a monkey. Some have managed to balance for a five count before falling but most never make it past two or three. Frequently, I'll repeat my instructions and give them another chance.

In all the years I have used this test only a handful of people have taken the staff, laid it flat on the floor, and stood on it, thereby keeping their feet off the floor. So what if they're only two inches off the floor. It sure is a lot easier than climbing a thin pole and attempting to balance on it. My point is this: many people make their problems far harder than they really are by not examining the constraints to see if they are really true. They focus so intently on what they perceive the problem and its constraints to be that they cannot solve even the simplest problem.

Have you heard of the Arthurian legend concerning the sword in the stone? Only young Arthur was able to remove the sword from its imprisonment in the rock and he thereby became king of all England. In the ancient East there was a similar legend concerning the Gordian Knot. Whoever could loose the impossibly convoluted knot, it was claimed, would rule all Asia. All who tried failed until a young soldier named Alexander came upon it. After failing to find a starting point to untie the knot, he said, "I guess I'll just have to make up my own knot-untying rules." With that he drew his sword and sliced the knot in half. Within a matter of a few short years all of Asia fell before the sword of Alexander the Great. He had simply discarded the constraints that the others felt they were under. With the constraints removed the solution to the problem was ridiculously easy and that's they way it often is.

At a recent seminar a young man stood up and told me that despite the fact that he wanted to make $100,000 a year running a small business, he lived in a very rural part of the state and simply did not have enough people in his area to make his dream a reality. I told him that for $99 Greyhound would take him anywhere he wanted to go. While you might think this answer was a little trite or obvious, believe me it is not. Many people simply do not consider obvious and simple answers to their problems because they place too many mental constraints on their thinking.

This country is a large and wonderful place. If you can't make a living doing what you want in one area, move closer to a major city in your state. Better still move to a fast growing area in the sunbelt like Nevada, Texas, Florida, or California. There is no reason on earth why you can't pack up and move, other than your own lack of desire to do so.

Step Three: Generate a Creative Solutions List

Once your problem has been clearly defined and broken into its components and the constraints have been listed it is time to solve the problem. This is the part that most people fail to perform correctly. Solution generation is a skill that is not passed on to you by your mother or father. You must develop this skill. As such, the more you practice, the better you get at it.

When faced with a difficult problem it is important that you don't allow yourself to be governed by rigid or straight-line thinking. That is what most people do because that is what they were taught to do. If you want to get ahead of them, you must think in three dimensions not in straight lines. You must allow your mind to wander in all directions and throw out any kind of wild and crazy solution that it cares to. You then write each idea down as it comes and go back later to analyze the particular merits of each.

Let's suppose that you have locked yourself out of your house. The first thing you would do is to call your spouse or in-laws to get a spare key. If that fails you could look for an open window on the ground floor. The adventurous might even borrow a ladder and try a second story window. That is probably as far as most people would go. So far the attack on the problem has been one-dimensional. Now let's look at the other possibilities. An open skylight on the roof or a chimney would allow you to approach the problem from above. A basement might allow you to approach the problem from below. Now the problem has been examined in more than three-dimensions. And, of course, if you needed to get into the house to rescue a child from a fire you would remove all mental constraints and smash a window. Problem solved!

During World War II the Germans turned a medieval castle into their highest security prisoner of war camp. It was reserved only for those allied prisoners who had escaped several times from regular POW camps. It stood impressively on a huge rock above the town and the Germans believed it to be escape proof.

Imagine for a moment that you are a prisoner of war in Colditz Castle. List five ways you can get out of such an impressive fortress.

1. _____
2. _____
3. _____
4. _____
5. _____

Did you think of tunneling out and climbing over thirty foot stone walls? What else did you come up with? How about pole vaulting over a barbed wire fence on the exercise field and running to freedom? How about strapping yourself to the underside of a delivery truck? What about the group who built a glider complete with catapult out of scrap material to launch it from a loft high up in one of the castle's towers? Pretty ingenious! The point is you must always look for unconventional and creative ways to solve your problems. One technique for doing this is called *reframing*.

REFRAME YOUR PROBLEMS

You have seen a picture of Leonardo da Vinci's famous painting, Mona Lisa, haven't you? It's a painting of a young woman with a curious smile. It is framed in an ornate gold leaf frame, hangs in the Louvre museum in Paris, France, and is one of the most valuable paintings in the world. The thing that has attracted people to that painting is the Mona Lisa's smile. Why is she smiling? Who is she smiling at? Nobody knows, but that doesn't stop them from speculating. What do you think it would do to the way people feel about the painting if it were removed from its ornate gold leaf frame and put in a more modern one. How about a bright red plastic frame about three inches wide with little pictures of Mickey Mouse and Donald Duck on it? The picture itself would remain unchanged, but what would that frame do to the way people looked at and felt about the painting?

The chances are it would dramatically change the way everyone saw the painting. Would you still think of it as a priceless work of art? Would it become more amusing or less amusing? My point is that reframing can change the way you look at a painting. And so it is with the many problems you face in life. Reframing them can have a wonderful effect on both your attitude toward them and your ability to solve them.

A problem is often as big or as small as you decide it is going to be. If the boss yells at you for doing something wrong you can tell yourself what a jerk he is. This will fill your mind with negativity and cause you a great deal of stress and anger. It will also affect your productivity. You will carry this poor attitude home with you in the evening and so you'll argue with your spouse, yell at the kids, and kick the dog. One episode has destroyed your entire day. Have you ever had a trivial thing ruin your whole day? Of course you have. We all have. But it doesn't have to get the better of you.

Try reframing this problem in a different way and and see if it doesn't produce far better results. Although you are upset both by your mistake and by your boss's poor attitude toward it you could look at the problem this way: "That was nice of him to correct me instead of firing me." Or think of how helpful of him it was to point out your mistakes so that you'll become a better worker and therefore make fewer mistakes in the future. This will enhance your worth and will lead to your making more money. Now I am not saying that it is easy to get yourself to do this, but I can guarantee you that if you try it will work. By reframing the situation in this light you will be able to maintain a good attitude and continue with your work throughout the day.

During the Battle of the Bulge, one of the most ferocious battles fought during World War II, an American commander by the name of McAuliffe and his troops were surrounded by the German army. The opposing general gave him the choice to surrender or be killed. He sent back a message to the German high command that said simply "Nuts."

When he addressed his men he told them that they had an opportunity unique in the annals of military history: They could attack the enemy in any direction they wished! Now that's reframing a situation.

Here are some other ways to enhance your ability to solve problems by using reframing techniques to approach the problem from someone else's point of view.

Avoid the Rut

Perhaps the greatest skill you can develop to speed up your path to the top is the ability to look at problems from outside yourself. Clear your mind of any thoughts, prejudices, or traditional procedures and pretend you are a ghost looking at yourself. Try to achieve a sense of objectivity and look at your situation in a new way.

Unsuccessful people come across a problem and then spend days, weeks, even years talking about the problem. "The economy's bad so I can't get a job," they say. It never occurs to them that talking about the problem does not produce results. It just digs the rut they are in deeper. In order to get out of the rut you must take a "what if" approach to each new obstacle. Instead of focusing on the problem try instead to focus on the solution. No matter how unlikely or stupid the solutions you come up with seem to be, keep throwing solutions at your problem until one comes up that makes sense. Do not allow conventional thinking to stop you from reaching a solution.

Peter's Lesson

A great example of this happened close to my home. A major two-lane street narrows to pass through a strange tunnel under the railway tracks. The tunnel is lined with tin and is about twenty-five yards long. One day to avoid a delay because of road construction a school bus driver decided to take this route instead of his normal path. When the bus reached the middle of the tunnel there was a loud screeching sound and the bus came to a stop. It was stuck. The driver tried to back out of the tunnel but with no success.

The children had to leave the bus through the rear emergency door, and the police were called. Unsure of what to do they called the fire department, which in turn called a large commercial tow truck. The tow truck was hooked to the back of the bus and pulled but the bus did not budge. The tow truck driver, a policeman, and a fire captain stood around and discussed the problem. They talked about cutting away some of the tunnel's tin lining, and someone suggested a second tow truck might help. As they walked around and around discussing the problem, a small boy named Peter walked up to the fire chief and tugged at his shirt. "Sir," he asked, "why don't you just let some of the air out of the tires and make the bus lower?" The captain smiled at the boy, then slowly walked into the tunnel to let the air out of the tires.

For almost a hour an army of grownups had looked at the problem and tried to force the bus out of the tunnel. But Peter had a better solution. Kids do not look at problems the same way adults do. They don't let things get in the way of their thinking. Looking at problems though the eyes of a child is actually a great way to solve them.

Think Like a Big Shot

Soon after I moved to California one of the large banks ran a credit card promotion that awarded customers points based on the amount of money they charged on their cards each month. The points could be redeemed for gifts in a catalog. One of the top prizes was a trip for two to Hawaii. I immediately set my sights on the trip and began spending up a storm. I charged gas, meals, computer equipment, and anything I could. At the end of the promotion I had charged up just enough points to make the trip.

I called the number to book my trip. The line was busy. I tried two or three times that day and the next with the same lack of success. After that I kept the number and prize brochure on the corner of my desk and continued to call at irregular intervals. Finally after about six months someone answered the phone. They politely informed me that the deadline to order prizes had passed ten days before. I explained that I could not get through and the operator informed me that the promotion had been far more successful than they had anticipated and a lot of other people had the same complaint. However, she told me she could do nothing. She suggested that I write a letter to the head office.

I did this fully expecting to get my trip and an apology for my inconvenience. Instead, I got a form letter telling me that I was too late to qualify for my trip. I wrote again and received back the same form letter. Now I was mad. I had spent over $40,000 to qualify for this trip and I wanted it.

I had called and I had written not one but two detailed letters and still no one took any action. At the time

I was running a small advertising agency and as I sat contemplating my problem I thought, "Now what could I do if I were a large agency?" I could run a campaign telling people all over America what a rotten bank they were. Yes, that was it! I could publicize their crime to everyone and get people to stop using their bank. But my company was small. What could I do against such a giant? Still, I thought it was worth a try.

I typed out a letter on my agency stationery that detailed the way I had been treated. I headed my letter: "XYZ Bank—A non-customer-service story." I enclosed with it a list of the magazines, newspapers, and TV and radio stations that I planned to send my ad to. I then went to the post office to get the address of every bank branch in the state. Next, I went to the library to get the names and titles of every corporate officer I could find, from the president on down. I mailed my letter out on Monday to over 200 people. By 9.30 A.M. the following day my problem was solved. I got my tickets and my trip to Hawaii. After trying to solve the problem by traditional means, I looked at how to solve it from the perspective of someone else—a big ad agency—and sure enough it worked.

Think Like a Famous Person

A friend of mine came to me with a problem about a fairly new used car he had bought that had broken down several times. The dealer had fixed his car seven times in just six months. My friend asked for his money back but the dealer refused. He then asked to trade it in on another car but they offered him 60 percent less than he had paid for the car just six months earlier. He was very frustrated with the situation and felt helpless. "What could he do to make them help him," he asked.

I told him that instead of looking at the situation through his eyes he should look at it as though he were someone else. For example, how would the famous consumer advocate, Ralph Nader, deal with the problem? After thinking for a few moments my friend decided that he would generate so much negative publicity that the dealership would be forced to fix the problem.

Now he had a new problem: How could he generate enough publicity to get the dealership to take notice of him? I told him to go home, take out a sheet of paper, write the problem at the top, and figure out all the possible ways he could generate publicity. He did and about an hour later he called back. It had worked. After writing down the problem he didn't even need to get to the solutions part. "You see," he said, "I wrote down 'My car is a lemon and I want it replaced by the dealership.' Well that was it!" he exclaimed. "Lemon!"

He went on to explain how he had driven to the dealership and asked to see the manger. He politely told him of the problems. The manager was sympathetic but offered no solution. He told the manager that if his car was not replaced for one of equal value he was going to mount a giant lemon on the roof of the car with the dealership's name on it and pay someone to drive it around the auto center every weekend until the problem was fixed. He was also going to call the local paper and news media to see if they wanted to take pictures. The manager quickly offered him an excellent trade on another car.

Play the "What If?" Game

When faced with a problem take out a blank sheet of paper and write the problem at the top of the page. Now start writing underneath it all the ways in which this problem could be solved. Do not think over your answers, just write all your ideas down no matter how silly or unlikely they seem. For example, suppose you need $20,000. Take a piece of paper and write the problem—A Lack of Capital: $20,000—at the top. Then brainstorm for possible solutions. Your list might included the following:

Get a loan from the bank

Ask Uncle Mort

Sell my car

Use my credit cards

Rob a bank

Win the lottery

Cash in my life insurance

Sell some of my stock

Get a partner for my venture

Remember, the key is not to think about the validity of the ideas as you write them. Just be free and write. When you have filled the entire page with possibilities, go back and cross off the ideas that really are off base. In the above list start by crossing off "Rob a bank" and "Win the lottery." Then let's just suppose the bank won't lend you money, so cross that off too. Continue examining the list, crossing off the impractical solutions. Eventually you're left with either getting a partner or asking Uncle Mort.

Now take a second piece of paper and head it "Finding a Partner." On this list all of your friends, business associates, and relatives and include other possibilities such as advertising in the newspaper. If you continue this process you will be amazed at the great ideas and solutions that you come up with. There is magic in letting your mind run free in What-If Land and in writing your thoughts down in black and white.

Change Your Problem-Solving Environment

A problem that seems insurmountable in your ten-by-ten office with the phone ringing and the computer humming will take on a whole new light when you drive alone to the beach or the lake and look at it again. Very few offices are set up to stimulate creative thinking. They have no quiet rooms, hang stock prints on the walls, and play elevator music twenty-four hours a day. It is very often necessary to take your problems out of this sterile environment and solve them elsewhere.

I personally find that very few major problems are solved in the office. Instead I solve many of my business problems, as well as those of my own, when I jog with my two dogs to the lake near my home. Jogging in itself makes me feel good physically, and it relieves tension as I run. Fatigue and stress are two of the most stifling causes of uncreative thinking. By jogging or doing some other such activity you are killing two birds with one stone. You are improving your cardiovascular system and increasing your stamina while at the same time relieving stress.

When I get to the lake and watch my dogs splash around in the water, it puts me in a dreamy sort of state where ideas begin to float into my mind. Try this yourself. Take a particular problem with you out of the office and into a different environment. You will be surprised how much more creative you become.

The office is rarely the best place to be creative, but why not do some creative thinking right now? Try thinking of how you could improve this situation. What could you do at the office to make it more interesting, even if it's only moving the furniture around and hanging your pictures on different walls? Change creates an air of excitement that helps people increase their creativity.

Improve Your Creativity with Experiment Day

If you examine your life you will find that in many ways you are incredibly predictable and set in your ways. I don't care whether you are a nineteen-year-old college student or a fifty-year-old corporate president. If you look at your life it is very predictable. You get up about the same time each day, drive the same way to work, and eat in the same small circle of restaurants. You watch the same TV shows each week, read the same magazines, and listen to the same radio station. Of course this type of behavior is not conducive to creative thinking. Instead it is rigid and boring. The good news is you can change it quickly by designating one day a week as Experiment Day.

Try designating Tuesday or Wednesday as Experiment Day because they are in the middle of the week when creativity is often at its lowest point. Get your spouse and friends involved in your experiment as well. There is only one rule and it is simple: On Experiment Day you do things differently than during the rest of the week.

Start off your day by getting up one hour earlier or staying in bed one hour later. If you normally read the newspaper in the morning, don't read it today. If you don't read the newspaper, read it! On Experiment Day take four or five things in your life that are constantly the same and change them. Drive to work taking a totally different route even if it's longer. You'll see different billboards, people, businesses, buildings, and real estate. Each new thing you encounter by taking a different route or changing your schedule may be an opportunity waiting to happen. A change of environment stimulates your mind and often brings opportunities into your life.

On your drive to work tune into a different radio station. If you usually listen to rock tune into a classical or talk station. If you listen to an oldies station change to rap and resist the temptation to turn it off after the first song. Stick it out until you get to work. If the songs are really bad you might even find yourself hoping that you get to work sooner so that you can turn it off! But that's good, too, because it forces you into a good attitude about getting to work.

At lunch go to a new restaurant. Then instead of ordering the usual burger and fries try something that you have never tasted before like blackened swordfish with cactus salsa. (Which is very good by the way.) On your way home instead of grabbing a video, pick up a copy of a magazine you have never read. Read it. It doesn't matter if you have any interest in the subject matter; that's not the point. In fact it is better if you pick up a magazine on a subject that may not interest you much. Perhaps pick out a flying or diving magazine, or one on model trains, horse riding, fishing, or travel. Spend the time you would have spent watching TV reading your magazine to gain more knowledge, insight, and ideas. I have often gleaned great ideas from reading magazines on subjects that bore no relation to anything that interests me while sitting in a waiting room. While you read, drink a different brand of beer or substitute fruit juice for your customary soda.

If you follow this simple plan of changing your routine and broadening your experience base just one day each week, you will be delighted by the new things you will find in your life. It is also amazing how simple little changes like this, done on a regular basis, can help increase your creativity.

List five key problems that are holding you back.

1. _____

2. _____

3. _____

4. _____

5. _____

Are they immediate problems? Put a "yes" or "no" next to them. Are they critical problems that, if not solved, will stall all other progress? List the constraints for each problem. Have you used a three-dimensional approach? Try solving them by reframing. Have you taken a piece of blank paper and played the What If game? Have you looked at them from a different person's perspective?

Resolve now to use the three step method each time you are faced with a problem. Then seek out new and creative ways to solve your problems using the techniques we have discussed and move on toward your goals.

LESSON 10

HOW TO MOTIVATE YOURSELF

Y ou can't sleep one night so you get up and turn on the TV. What's on? Probably an old rerun, a detective story. Maybe it's Kojack, Columbo, or McCloud—it doesn't matter, pick your favorite. Whoever you watch is on a manhunt for a murderer, right? The detective has some evidence and several suspects. There is one suspect, however, who does not have a good alibi for the night the murder took place. One key question remains unanswered; it is always the same one. Do you know what it is? "What was the murderer's motive?" Was the crime committed for revenge, money, or love? Just as the TV detectives are always looking for an answer to this question, so you too must find the answer as it applies to your life.

WHAT'S YOUR MOTIVATION?

What are the key factors that motivate you? Do you know exactly what they are? Or what about your employees?

What motivates them? What about your spouse? Your children? Do you know what motivates them to higher performance?

All too often the answer is not clear. Having read this far, you now know many of the skills you must develop or fine tune in order to make it to the top. However, all these will be wasted if you can't motivate yourself to put them into action. While it is easy to talk about success, it is much more difficult to put in the work needed to achieve it.

For all but the successful, motivation is a very elusive concept. Successful people seem to be able to motivate themselves into action no matter what is going on around them. In fact, very often the negative things around them motivate them even more. In this lesson we are going to explore some of the many different techniques that successful people use to get the "Get Up and Go" into their lives.

LIFE'S TWIN MOTIVATORS

There are basically just two motivational forces at work in the whole world. Pleasure and pain. We do anything to gain pleasure and everything to avoid pain. Many successful people have made it big through a burning desire to leave the poverty of their childhood behind them. They use the poverty and hopelessness of their upbringing in the cities and ghettos to fuel their fire for success. Others who needed money for a medical operation to keep a loved one alive but were unable to provide the needed funds are driven to never again be in such a helpless position. Some people find that their physical handicap becomes the driving force, believing that they must work harder in life to prove their worth. These are all examples of negative motivation—people driven to achieve to avoid pain and frustration.

Life is full of goals to achieve, challenges to meet, and obstacles to overcome along the way. Whether these goals, challenges, and obstacles are successfully dealt with often depends on the level of motivation of the person facing them.

A Tale of Two Cities Revisited

Two people I know in the martial arts business grew up in the same town in the Midwest. Dan and John met when they started taking karate lessons at twelve years of age at the same studio. They went to the same high school and became best friends. They went to the same college and both passed with higher than average scores. They were young, good looking, and full of dreams. Recently they met at their high school's ten-year reunion. Right after college, their parents had moved to opposite ends of the state, so they had not been in frequent contact with each other. Their lives, however, were still remarkably similar. After college each had moved to towns similar in size and had taken various jobs to make a few bucks. After a couple of years, each had saved enough to open his own karate studio. Both married, and both were expecting a child later that year. They could hardly believe they were following such similar paths in life.

While their paths were virtually identical, the results were not. Dan's studio had 50 paying clients, John's had 250. Dan struggled to pay the rent on a one-bedroom apartment and John had a five-bedroom house with a pool. Dan's beat-up pickup leaked oil while John's black Corvette convertible sparkled in the sunlight. Dan's wife waited tables in a coffee shop to make ends meet; John's wife worked part-time helping several local charities on the days she was not at the tennis club.

Perhaps you know a similar story from your own experience, people you knew in high school, college, or business who in a very short time ended up at opposite ends of life. And perhaps you have wondered many times how it is that two equally talented people could come up with such stunningly different results? What gives one guy an edge in life over someone else?

The answer is motivation!

What motivates you? Is it money? A sense of achievement? Self-respect? Few people are actually motivated by money, although many think they are. Most people are motivated by a sense of self-respect or achievement. This is confirmed in surveys of the very successful. In fact money often appears way down their list of motivational factors. Instead they want others to think of them as successful people or as people to look up to and respect. When people reach this type of position in life the money usually follows as a byproduct.

Over forty years ago Abraham Maslow put forward his hierarchy of human needs. They can be summed up in three simple categories.

1. Basic needs—those of air, food, and water
2. Social needs—such as love and the feeling of security
3. Self-actualization needs—the need to fulfill one's unique potential

The true source of an individual's motivation often does not appear until it is questioned. For example, take the man who says he is motivated by money. When you ask him what he would do with the money he says he would buy a new Ferrari. You ask him why he wants a Ferrari and he has to think for a moment before answering. Then he tells you it's because people who own Ferraris are successful people. They park them up front at restaurants and, beside, their neighbors have fits of envy. What is really important to this man is not the money or the Ferrari, instead he really craves the feeling of respect and importance that they provide.

What motivates a woman to pay large sums of money for tiny bottles of perfume? Because they smell good is always the first answer. But is it really the smell that motivates her to buy? Not really. Face it, a perfume that costs $200 does not smell that much different from one that costs $50. The woman is not motivated by the smell but by the feelings she expects that smell to arouse in her. Feelings like being beautiful, of increased self-esteem, of being loved and being in love, and of confidence. The greater the price of the perfume the greater the feelings she associates with it.

By asking yourself a series of questions you can discover your true motivation in life. You can then use this knowledge to create pressure on yourself to perform. "Wait a minute!" you say. "What do you mean I can create *pressure* on myself? That's what I want to get rid of!" Well that is not necessarily true. Not all pressure is bad and some pressure is good. Good pressure is the type of pressure you use to motivate yourself into action.

Let me give you an example of good pressure. You decide that you are going to be the number one salesperson in your division. At your weekly meeting you stand up in front of your boss and your co-workers and announce this to everyone. Just to make sure that everyone heard you the first time you might want to mention it more than once. Now you have created pressure on yourself to meet those goals. You don't lie, right? You don't want to look stupid in front of your boss and co-workers, right? So what are your options now? To get it in gear and get moving!

Use the pressure you have created to motivate yourself into action. If you succeed in reaching your goal you will gain the praise of your boss, thus boosting your self-esteem. You will also be esteemed by your peers, avoiding the pain of looking bad and also adding to your self-esteem. And you'll gain financially.

If you are a manager you will find this is an excellent method of getting results from your employees. Instead of placing pressure on them, help them create their own positive pressure. This will pay off in their careers as well as

in yours. Practice putting positive pressure on yourself
and encourage those around you to do the same.

POSITIVE AND NEGATIVE MOTIVATION

There are two ways in which you can motivate yourself
and others to reach goals. First, there is positive motivation in which you promise a reward for reaching a goal.
For example, you might promise yourself a new car,
home, or improved lifestyle. This is intended to get you
excited and motivated to work hard. In this case your motivation is provided by the rewards you will receive for
your efforts.

Second there is negative motivation. Negative motivation occurs when you dwell on all the bad things that
will happen if you do not achieve your goal. If you don't
work harder the boss may fire you. If you don't find a better job you might lose your house and you will never be
able to send the kids to college. Negative motivation drives
you to succeed by confronting you with your fear of failure.
Think of it as moving away from failure as opposed to
moving toward success.

Refer back to Lesson Three and look at your number
one goal. List five positive things that will occur when you
reach it.

1. _____
2. _____
3. _____
4. _____
5. _____

Now list five negative or painful things that will come
into your life if you do not achieve this goal.

1. _____
2. _____
3. _____
4. _____
5. _____

You now have five negative and five positive reasons to achieve your number one goal. Which one gives you the greatest sense of motivation? Positive or negative? Both types of motivation can be extremely effective in helping you reach your goals and there is no reason you can't use both to get in gear. It does not matter whether you use positive or negative motivation just as long as you get motivated to achieve more in your life.

You should have been able to identify which type of motivation works best for you. Now use some of the following techniques in order to heighten that sense of motivation. The more motivated you are to get ahead the faster you will achieve your goals.

LIVE YOUR DREAMS FOR A FEW MINUTES EACH DAY

The great majority of people who grew up in an average home often find it difficult to develop the burning desire and motivation necessary to reach the top. One reason many people are not highly motivated to achieve the most out of their lives is very simple. They have no experience of the pain, anger, and desperation of poverty that has driven so many people to the top, and their experience of the best things in life is limited to half an hour of Robin Leach on *Lifestyles of the Rich and Famous*. They are lost in the comfort zone, leading average American lives.

In order to develop positive motivation you need to see what you are missing and experience some of these things, so you can actually take in the sights, sounds, smells, and feelings of success. This will help you develop the motivation to pursue them in order to have them as part of your everyday experience in the future.

How can you get truly excited and motivated about something if you have no idea how it will improve your life? How does it feel to play the world's best golf courses, ski the Alps, or sail a yacht in Bermuda? Do you know? Do your goals seem too lofty to even bother starting? If they do, then bring them closer to home.

If you have never left your home state how can you know the sights and sounds that you are missing in Paris or Rome? You must expand your horizons further afield to take in more of life. Don't get trapped in a small town mentality; there is a wide and wonderful world out there just waiting for you to come and visit.

If you lack motivation, it's time to remind yourself what success feels like. Try this this little exercise: Dress up in your best clothes, get your hair cut, make reservations at the finest restaurant in town, hire a limousine for the night, and take out your spouse or friend on a date. Take in every detail of the experience: the limousine driver calling you "sir," the maître d' taking you to the best table, the excellent service and exquisite food. Relish the wine, the ambiance, and the feeling of success it all creates. Etch this experience in your mind so that you'll remember exactly how good it feels to be treated like a king. You will surely want more. I don't care if you have to eat at home for the next two months in order afford this one evening out. Do it!

If you have always dreamed of owning a Corvette or Ferrari go and drive one. What is stopping you? Make your dream real. Feel, smell, and drive it. There are companies all over the country that rent exotic cars for the day. So it may cost you a week's wages or more for a day behind the wheel of the car of your dreams, but that's okay. Once you have felt the power of the car and the way it handles and have experienced the pleasure you get from the way people stare when you drive by you will want to experience all this again. If spending that much money for a one-day ride seems over your head, join the local chapter of the Ferrari Club and attend a local meeting. There you are bound to meet someone who will let you enjoy the experience for free.

Instead of going to Florida for two weeks every year spend this summer in Europe. See Rome, Paris, or London. Get a look at other peoples and cultures. It does not matter whether it's cars, homes, restaurants, or whatever. Pick some experience that gets you closer to the things you want in life and make that experience spur you on to greatness. It works.

I have frequently used this technique to motivate myself. When I was making less than $350 a week I spent more than that to stay for one night at the Boulders resort in Carefree, Arizona. I saw a picture of the hotel and golf course in a magazine and just had to go. I enjoyed it so much that I spent a second night. It took me several weeks to pay for this short trip. But the wonderful feelings and pictures I took back home spurred me on for months toward making the kind of income I needed to vacation in places like that several times a year.

ANCHORING

First discovered by Doctor Ivan Pavlov, anchoring is a widely used technique to help people reach peak states of emotional and mental performance. Anchoring is used to quickly recall a stimuli and create a feeling in the mind that spurs it into action. In Pavlov's original experiments he would ring a bell when feeding hungry dogs. This bell anchored a pleasurable state in the minds of the dogs. In a very short time Pavlov had only to ring the bell to get the dogs salivating wildly despite the absence of food.

You already have some anchors both positive and negative built into your mind. Do you know what they are? Have you ever received bad news late at night on the telephone? Every time the phone rings late at night now there is a good chance that it will immediately trigger anxiety in you because of your negative anchor. Your heart probably beats faster, you might become jittery, and you may even stop breathing briefly so you can listen.

For our purposes we are interested in positive anchors or a memorable experience that will heighten your motivation. Try this now: Think back to a time when you felt great about something. Maybe you won a contest, got a promotion, passed a key examination, or had a great vacation. Remember how it felt to be a winner. Remember how you felt swimming in the warm tropical water—relaxed, happy, great. Now look at yourself in the mirror as you anchor your mind on this pleasant memory. Are you smiling? Are you sitting up a little straighter? Do you feel more relaxed? Do you feel more excited than you did just a few seconds ago? You should.

With just a little practice you can quickly use these past positive experiences as driving forces to help motivate you to reach even better ones in the future. At the beginning of every new golf season golfing legend Jack Nicklaus would watch movies of his past successes to anchor him to a positive state and motivate him for the year. He used anchoring to remind himself how great it was to win. This motivated him to go out and practice to sharpen his game so he could win and feel great again.

MAKE A VIDEO OF YOU MOTIVATING YOU

You can use an idea similar to Nicklaus's to motivate yourself. All you need to do is to make a video of yourself motivating yourself. Set up a camera and get ready to have fun.

Pick a time of the day and a week when you are definitely feeling up, when things are going well, and when the future looks bright. Then film yourself in this state, saying all the right words and doing all the right things that you know will hit your own personal hot buttons.

In this video, talk about the future, about things that get you excited, things that you are feeling at the time of the video taping. Talk about how things have changed for the better up to that point and how things are going to keep getting better in the future. In short, be your own coach. Tell yourself, out loud, what you need to in order to feel up.

When you feel down or unmotivated simply throw in the tape and let yourself motivate yourself. The tape should serve as a very effective anchor. It may sound a bit odd, but it works. That's all that counts; whatever it takes to get you moving is what you need to do.

If you don't have a video camera you can still get yourself feeling good about your life and the people around you by watching uplifting movies. Try movies like *Rocky* that get you cheering or others like *E.T.*, *Arthur,* or *Cocoon* that leave you with a warm glow and feeling good about life. Once you achieve that warm state remember it and store it for when you need a boost. When you feel down rent the tape to get you going again.

Music Is a Great Motivator

Once you have a positive experience you must anchor it in your mind so that it can be recalled to motivate you into action when needed. Have you ever heard a song on the radio and suddenly felt happy or sad? This is anchoring in action. A song that was playing on the radio when your first love said goodbye could be forever burned in your mind as a negative memory and therefore as a negative anchor. Remember the movie *Casablanca*? Remember "As Time Goes By," the song Rick wouldn't let Sam the piano player play because it reminded him of his lost love?

Every time you hear your "done-me-wrong" song it takes your mind directly back to that fateful event and you immediately feel sad and depressed. Sometimes this happens to you and you don't know why. Suddenly you feel down for no reason. Very often this will be because of some kind of subconscious negative anchor. If you think about it you may be able to recall the negative event that coincided with the playing of this song. Hearing the song takes you back to experience the same mental, emotional, and physical condition that you were in when you anchored this particular event in your mind.

This also works in a positive manner in the case of a song that was played night and day on the radio that certain summer when you had a blast. As soon as that song comes on, you are suddenly back in the summer of '69, quietly smiling to yourself and feeling suddenly happy.

When I was fourteen or fifteen years old a group called the Boomtown Rats (led by Bob Geldoff who founded the whole Live Aid organization) had the number one song in England. The song was called "Rat Trap" and although I never even came close to the situation described in the song—a young man's desperation to break out of his hopeless situation—the desperation in the song inspired me "You can make it if you want to or you need it bad enough." Every time I heard that song I drew energy from it, got excited, and bore down even harder on whatever I was doing. As time went by there were other songs that also helped to pump me up. I would buy the record and then record the song on a separate tape. Soon I had both sides of a cassette filled with the type of songs that fired me up. I would play this tape on the way to golf tournaments and later before business meetings and seminars. By the time I was though listening to these tapes I felt like a million bucks no matter what else was going on.

Buy or record those songs that anchor you in a positive manner and keep the tape handy to be played whenever you feel yourself drifting toward a negative attitude. If you sit up straight, smile, and play some key tunes it is impossible to feel down or unmotivated.

Anchoring on songs is easy and there are hundreds of different ways to anchor yourself. When I looked closely at the gestures I use when I am excited I found that I clench my right fist and move it quickly up and down. I do this when I hit a great shot on the golf course, when I close a large deal over the phone, or when I respond to any number of other positive events. In order to fire myself up I only have to clench my fist and move it up and down fast. If I also shout "Yeah!" as I make this gesture it heightens my state even further. When I use this simple anchor, I feel strong, excited, healthy, and motivated all at once.

Watch yourself. What types of gestures or words do you use when good things are happening to you? Once you have discovered what works, develop your anchor so you can use it to alter your mental state and increase your motivation.

Do What You Like

People commonly tell me that they hate their jobs. "I'm burned out!" they announce. "What can I do?" Well, what can you do? What are you good at, or more importantly what do you like to do? I can tell you that once your enthusiasm for a business or job is lost you are fighting a losing battle. It is far better to cut your losses and move on than to continue in a life you do not enjoy. Life is indeed far too short to spend a good deal of it involved in something you do not like. It is absolutely impossible to motivate yourself for any decent length of time to do something you do not enjoy doing.

Over 80 percent of highly successful people would choose to work in the same field again. This is not because they became successful in this field but because they enjoy their work so much that they could throw themselves into it and therefore become successful.

Take inventory of your skills and list them below. Are you good at selling? Are you good with people? Are you a good talker? A good listener? Do you speak another language? Are you creative?

1. _____
2. _____
3. _____
4. _____
5. _____
6. _____
7. _____
8. _____
9. _____
10. _____

Now list the ten things you enjoy most. For example, golfing, fishing, reading, traveling, writing, animals, etc.

1. _____
2. _____
3. _____
4. _____
5. _____
6. _____
7. _____
8. _____
9. _____
10. _____

Now try to match one of your key talents with one of the activities that you most enjoy. If it happens that you are good with people and like to fish consider opening up a bait shop, running a charter service for fishermen, or selling fishing equipment to tackle stores. If you like to travel you could work for an airline or a cruise line or perhaps open your own travel agency. As with laying out your goals the most important part of this exercise is to approach it in a totally uninhibited way. Do not think right now of all the negative reasons why you may not be able to do what you want. Instead, focus only on matching your skills with the activities you love. Let your mind run free to the wide range of possibilities that exist for you.

If you love golf as I do you could work at a golf club in management, buy a franchise selling golf equipment, start a service running tournaments, sell clubs for a manufacturer, or start a repair service in your area. You could even go to school at night to become a golf course architect. Why not form a limited partnership and buy your own course? There are many part of the country where you can buy a course for a little more than a million dollars. With 20 percent down and a few partners that's just like buying a house. There are 101 other realistic and profitable ways you could be involved in the activity that you enjoy. But you need to start with a little uninhibited thinking.

Many of my friends have done these very things in order to do what they love. My good friend Dan Poppers left a high school teaching post to start a small bimonthly magazine in Palm Springs called *Golf News*. Golf is his passion and he loves the Palm Springs area. It took some time but now his magazine is a high-gloss, highly successful monthly respected throughout the industry. His position as editor affords him all kinds of perks like free golf and travel, all because he combined his talent of writing with his love of golf. Do you think he enjoys going to work in the morning? Of course he does because each new day is a chance to meet other golfers, play new courses, and interview top professionals.

Then you have the other side of the coin. I know a young man who works in the machining industry. He does not like his job; he knows that is just a matter of time before he is laid off because the plant is being shut down. His passion in life? He loves books and loves reading. So why doesn't he buy a bookstore franchise or start his own used bookstore? Wouldn't that make him look forward to every day? You bet it would. And yet something holds him back. It's not a lack of capital since it takes very little to open a used bookstore. Maybe it's fear of failure, maybe it's a fear of the unknown—whatever it is he will not be truly happy until he confronts his problem and puts his effort into a career he enjoys.

Remember, it does not matter how young or how old you are. There is no reason not do what you want to do. You will reach the top far faster doing something that you like. There are a lot of opportunities out there and if you can't find one make one. You *can* make them. Take a look at your present situation. Are you doing the type of work you really want to do? If you answered "No!" then it is time to take stock of your talents and reevaluate the possibilities that are out there waiting for you.

What is your passion? Follow it! Get the most from your life! When you are excited about what you are doing it not only pays off for you but it stimulates those around you too.

Do what you like to do. Combine that with what you do best. Now do it better than anyone ever has. Do I sound overly simplistic? Instead of thinking how improbable it sounds think of how much fun it will be. Imagine waking up every day to do something you love and to do it with the skill you do best. Wouldn't that make your life better very quickly? Wouldn't you work harder, faster, and more productively doing something you loved every single day? Don't you think that following your passion would get you to your goals faster than any other route?

USE PHYSIOLOGY TO KEEP YOUR EMOTIONS IN BALANCE

Your emotional state and how you manage it also plays a large part in your motivation. If you feel depressed or angry you can't work at peak efficiency and therefore do not move toward your goals rapidly (if indeed you move toward them at all). People who reach the top generally have good control of their emotions.

Emotional states are very closely linked to physiology. The easiest way to put yourself in a positive frame of mind is to sit up straight and smile. It is physically impossible to feel down when in this position. It is also impossible to feel good when you are hunched over your desk with a frown on your face.

Have you ever noticed how successful people seem to give off an aura of success? You can tell by their dress, mannerisms, and attitude that they have made it. They look important because they feel important. Successful people stand and sit up straight. They walk a little faster than most people, they talk a little faster, they get work done faster, and they reach the top faster. They have important things to do, so why wait around? They smile more or at least seldom seem to frown. Successful people look like they are up most of the time. That's because they are. You can't make it in any endeavor if you are feeling sorry for yourself.

The next time you feel down just sit up straight, smile, and do things a bit faster. You will find that as soon as you take on the physical posture of someone who is not down you will not be down—it is physically impossible. This change of feeling can be of great help in keeping your motivation going.

Watson's Lesson

Although I have been out of college less than ten years and I have a reasonable memory I can only recall the name of one of my professors. By my third semester I had already run out of courses that I really wanted to take, so I found myself enrolling in both English literature and American literature classes in the same term.

Now, although I love reading I must confess that the prospect of studying English literature and the works of Shakespeare, Milton, Coleridge, and others long since dead held little joy for me. I felt much better about studying American literature and figured I'd enjoy that class more. But the truth was that in the end when a friend asked me what I had studied in that class all I could remember was Twain's story about the jumping frogs of Calaveras County and the Robert Frost poem "Nothing Gold Can Stay," both of which I had read several months prior to actually taking the class.

With my English literature class the story was completely different. I can still remember professor Watson B. Duncan dancing over the stage with surprising grace despite his advancing years. I can hear him yelling lines from Milton's *Paradise Lost*, "Threw him headlong flaming from the ethereal sky!" he would roar with the passion of an accomplished actor while he threw his arms around wildly. He referred to William Shakespeare simply as "The Big S."

His classes were so popular that they were held in the auditorium. One day when I entered the room I found it almost pitch black, yet with everyone already in their seat. Suddenly a spotlight shone on the stage. Professor Duncan appeared and he asked if we knew what day it was. After all the obvious answers were exhausted he pulled back the curtains to reveal a giant cake complete with several hundred candles. "Today," he announced, "is The Big S's birthday! Come up and get some cake!"

Duncan was in his late sixties, of average height, and a little overweight. He wore square glasses and had a shock of bright white hair making him look a little like Einstein. He was not the type of man you would expect could relate to a bunch of kids a quarter of his age. He was a scholarly man and knew his subject intricately as did a lot of other professors on campus whose names and teaching I have long since forgotten. People did not forget Watson B. Duncan, though. No one cut his classes and they didn't fall asleep in the back row. In fact, people used to sneak into class just to hear him.

Duncan knew the key to teaching, unshakable enthusiasm. Enthusiasm oozed from him via his mannerisms, his tone of voice, and his words. Although many of the students were working two jobs and were out late the night before, when we left his class we felt recharged and revitalized. Watson B. Duncan had more enthusiasm than anyone I have ever met. We were helpless under his spell. Make his spell work for you!

Remember these key thoughts regarding enthusiasm:

- Enthusiasm goes hand in hand with a good attitude.
- Enthusiasm is contagious and spreads like wildfire.
- Enthusiasm makes up for a multitude of deficiencies in skill or knowledge.
- Enthusiasm attracts people to you.
- Enthusiasm opens doors closed to others.
- Enthusiasm is possessed by all successful people.

There is a karate instructor in Ohio who had purchased one of my business manuals. I called him to see how it had helped him. He answered the phone like this, "Hello! It's a great day here at XYZ TKD!" Now this is a standard method of answering the phone recommended by a training company in the industry, so I had heard it many time before. The difference was that he was the first person I had ever heard who really sounded like he meant what he said. He made it sound like Ohio was the place to be, this was the place I wanted to take martial arts lessons, and he was the person with whom I wanted to be involved. He spoke just one simple sentence with meaning and enthusiasm and I was sold. Develop this kind of enthusiasm for yourself, your job, your life, and your future. It will motivate you and the others around you to do what must be done in order to achieve your goals.

Resolve not to get down no matter what happens. Stay motivated and you will achieve your goals.

LESSON 11

TAKING ACTION

The future is there for those that take it.
— ELEANOR ROOSEVELT

PROCRASTINATION IS THE ENEMY

The very first seminar I taught was aimed at small business owners. At the end of the seminar five people came up to me to tell my how much they had enjoyed the seminar. Each then proceeded to describe in detail how they had been planning for several years to do exactly what I was doing. Two of the five even suggested that I could improve the quality of my seminar if I allowed them to help me. I asked both to send me a letter detailing their basic ideas. Neither letter ever arrived.

At my next seminar several weeks later a similar thing happened only this time six people approached me either immediately after the seminar or later that evening in private. Since then hardly a seminar goes by where at least one person does not tell me exactly the same thing: "I have been thinking about doing seminars on such and such." "Are you an expert on that subject?" I ask. "Oh yes!"

they say, "I have been involved in that field for twenty years." "Then why don't you do it?" I ask.

It is at that point that these people become truly creative, coming up with amazing reasons why they just can't begin teaching seminars right now. If they put half as much effort into figuring out creative solutions to real obstacles as they do in coming up with creative reasons to procrastinate there would be absolutely no chance of their failure. To my knowledge none of the people who has told me about his or her plans has ever actually gone ahead with them.

Have you ever been sitting in a coffee shop or a restaurant and overheard two people talking about all the things they were going to do just a soon as they:

had more money?

had more time?

quit their lousy job?

got a lucky break?

found someone else to help?

There simply is no disease more fatal to success than procrastination. It nips in the bud every best laid plan. Procrastination is known by cancerous little statements like, "I am tired. I'll do it later." "I will start right after the holidays are over." "When I finish this course, then I will be ready to get going." "I just felt like doing something else today. I will get to it next week, next month, next year." "I'll do it when I save up some more money."

You can find these and 1001 other excuses just like them on the lips of the millions who are not happy with their position in life. They are the wanna-be's trapped in a mediocre life that they really want to leave. Unfortunately for them, it seems that they are not unhappy enough to destroy their tendency toward procrastination. They can always find reasons why they should not start something right now. But if they gave their brains equal time to think of reasons why they should they would undoubtedly find just as many reasons to do it now. Are you in the same boat? Get going! Start! Lights, cameras, action! You cannot reach your goals without taking direct and immediate action to get you there.

WHY PEOPLE PROCRASTINATE

Do you procrastinate? If so, do you know why? What stops you from taking action toward your dreams? Dreams don't change the world; actions change the world. Procrastination really goes back to poor planning. If you have correctly laid out your goals and the actions needed to achieve them there should be no reason not to move forward. You have clearly identified the things you wish to achieve and the steps needed to accomplish them. You have set out a timetable, a check up system, and a reward system for reaching your short-term goals. You have no reason not to take action.

Generally, people procrastinate because they have not sat down and planned a course of action. They also procrastinate because the thought of leaving where they are now to move forward terrifies them. It terrifies them because they do not know what they will encounter along the way. They have not faced up to their fears. It is like having to walk through a pitch-black tunnel full of open manholes. They have no idea what they will encounter and so they do not even enter the tunnel.

If you have completed the planning stages, you can step boldly forward into the blackness. You know that you can expect manholes and you know you have made plans to deal with them when they come. You also know that what is on the other side of the tunnel is worth reaching. You know that the pain of not reaching your goals is far too great to stand still and do nothing. You also know that the rewards are great and if you stick to your plan over the long run there is no chance of failure.

Have you written down your goals yet? Have you drawn up a list of people you need to meet? Have you listed the actions and the dates by which your goals will be accomplished?

If the answer is no to any of these questions, then there is a very good chance that you are not ready to take the action needed to propel you to the top. Go back to lessons 3 and 4 on goal setting and planning and write out your goals. Complete your master plan for success before you continue reading this lesson.

It is amazing how the simple act of defining a clear plan and strategy will improve your life. You know, as I write this lesson I am filled with an intense feeling of excitement. By writing about the techniques I have used, it heightens my awareness of them and makes my own goals and strategies crystal clear. This clear picture of both the outcome and the actions needed to achieve this desired outcome will allow you to triumph over procrastination.

THE POWER OF ONE

You have all heard the well-worn phrase "knowledge is power," but knowledge is only potential power until it is actualized. A person with the knowledge to succeed who takes no action is no better off than a person with no knowledge at all.

A good example of the power of action horribly underused is the power to change government officials. You can change the direction of your city, county, state, or country by just casting your vote. Everybody knows this and yet around 40 percent of voters never make it to the polls when election day rolls around. Those who don't vote are often those who complain the loudest throughout the year about how bad the government is. They offer excuses why they didn't vote like, "I was busy that day" or "my one vote won't make any difference."

Let's look at how the action of just one person voting has changed the course of history. In 1645 one vote gave Oliver Cromwell control of England. In 1776 one vote gave America the English language instead of German. Think about it, if that one person hadn't voted you would be reading this book in German. *Ach du lieber!* In 1878 one vote gave Rutherford B. Hayes the presidency of the United States. In 1923 one vote gave Adolph Hitler the leadership of the Nazi party. One person could have saved the world from the Second World War.

All action, no matter how small, made in the right direction makes a difference. In life everything counts. Every single time you take action toward your goals you are lessening the time you will have to wait before realizing your ultimate reward. Conversely, every time you decide instead to delay action for another time you are ensuring that your ultimate prize gets further away.

ACTION CREATES OPPORTUNITY

People will often tell you that they are waiting for the right opportunity to come along before they will act. Perhaps they are waiting for a business that may come up for sale at just the right price. In reality, however, they are disappointed to find that prices keep rising. Or maybe they are waiting for another corporate officer to leave the company so that they can take his position. Instead, he stays until he drops dead on his eighty-ninth birthday. These people fail to realize that action must create opportunity, not the other way around.

Taking action is like generating a magnetic force that draws opportunity into your path. Do not get caught in the cycle of doing as little as possible. Show up at work a little earlier in the morning and leave a little later in the evening than everyone else and you will soon be noticed for that action if nothing else. Be creative within your work environment, always looking to create more opportunity for yourself by taking action rather than by avoiding it. Help others further their goals (especially your boss!) and you will be furthering you own goals faster than you thought possible.

Often if you are ready for action opportunities will present themselves in the most unusual ways and you will find yourself involved in new and interesting endeavors. While studying karate I learned that the school I studied at was going to get together with several others and hold a large tournament. I asked the organizers if they were going to have a program for the tournament. They said no. I then asked if I could make one up for them and sell ads to pay for it. They agreed, provided I was willing to split the money with them. This seemed like a reasonable arrangement and so I set out to develop one. It was a fairly crude attempt, ten pages photocopied on colored paper and stapled in the middle. It was, however, very well received because all the competitors got to see their name in print. I collected over $3,000 in advertising money. I paid someone to do the typesetting and copying for $500 and someone else to sell ads on commission. The net result was that I split almost $2,000 for doing very little. Now any one of the one thousand or so people in the tournament could have done what I did, but only I did it. You have to act on ideas to make them happen.

Sometimes where nothing exists you can create your own opportunity. Action always has a way of increasing opportunity, while procrastination and inaction always inhibit success.

Several years ago I decided to start my own golf tournament so I printed up some flyers, bought some trophies, and started putting it together. The first year I broke even on the actual event and secured a $6,000 advertising consulting job from one of the competitors. The second year I made $1,500 and made some excellent media contacts that I later used on other projects. The tournament took little effort after the first event and in one way or another it has paid off handsomely for me. Again, anyone can run a golf tournament and make money doing it. It is just a question of doing it. What's more, both of the examples above are tied to things I enjoy doing: karate and golf. It is possible to do the things you truly enjoy and make money and interesting connections through doing them. All you need to do is turn your ideas into action.

The ability to take action quickly and decisively is yet another mark of successful people. They can weigh the information in front of them and act on it without undue hesitation. A poor decision made quickly and decisively will often be better than no decision at all. In his autobiography Lee Iacocca wrote that if he had to sum up in one word what qualities make a successful manager it would all boil down to decisiveness: "You can use the fanciest computers in the world, gather all the charts and numbers, but in the end you have to bring all the information together, set up a timetable and act!"

INACTION IS OFTEN FATAL

Inaction is far more likely to kill your dreams than is action. A classic example of this is found in the period immediately before the Second World War. The Nazis had invaded Czechoslovakia, Austria, and most of Poland before British Prime Minister Neville Chamberlain's lack of action finally caused him to be removed from office. America herself stood by as almost all of Europe fell under the brutal Nazi regime. It took Pearl Harbor to wake her up and get her into action. Do not wait until your own personal Pearl Harbor happens. It may be too late to achieve your objectives by that time.

One of the most vivid memories that many of Winston Churchill's secretaries recalled after the war was that of a simple red stamp. On it were just three words; three powerful, meaningful words. When they where stamped in red ink at the top of a document people jumped to get things done. These simple words epitomized the difference between Churchill and Chamberlain. The words on the stamp were *Action This Day!* Make those words your words and you will find that you have found yet another key to reaching your goals.

The Importance of Setting Deadlines

Set deadlines for yourself to get things done. Make positive statements like, "I will review all the information I can and then make a decision by Friday at noon." Reward yourself in a small way once you have acted by having some coffee or getting a snack. Also set up a penal system for yourself. If you don't take action by the date you set fine yourself $10 and send it to your favorite charity.

When you go into a meeting resolve to get a decision on each of your major discussion points. If a lack of information stops you from making that decision, set a time for getting the information and then set another date for a decision. Better still don't go into any meeting without all the tools you need. Once you have set a deadline stick to it; make a decision and then go on to something else. If you get in the habit of making deadlines and keeping them your life will roll along toward your goals a lot more smoothly.

Get in Motion

There is a major scientific theory that goes along these lines "An object in motion, once in motion, tends to remain in motion until acted on by another force." So let's use this principle to put your life and dreams into action. Often the action needed to achieve your goals seems overwhelming and because of this it is easy to procrastinate.

In the case of Prime Minister Chamberlain, taking action to halt Hitler's advance would have resulted in a very painful state called war. Chamberlain chose procrastination because war was something he desperately wanted to avoid. However, when viewed with 20/20 hindsight, procrastination, as it almost always does, proved to be the wrong decision and in the end resulted in far more painful consequences. Britain ended up engaged in a war with its enemy far closer to its shore than it had been just a few weeks earlier, thus making the cost of winning far greater.

In your own personal life the easiest way to make large-scale changes is to first take small actions that get you in motion. Once the motion has started then other actions will become easier to take. As the saying goes "The journey of a thousand miles begins with the first step." Once you have taken that first step the next step becomes easier.

For example, suppose you have to read a report in order to make a key decision on another project. The report is long and boring and you just can't get into it at all. Take the report out and read the first section only. Allow yourself fifteen minutes, then put it away. Don't look at it again until tomorrow. This will allow you to get started on the report and the pain will last a very manageable fifteen minutes instead of two hours. Once you have started to read you may go on further if you wish, but your only commitment is for fifteen minutes. As soon as the fifteen minutes are up you can file the report if you wish, now with one section read. Then begin another task. By limiting your pain to just a few minutes then starting a new task it makes the discomfort much more acceptable to you. Often you will find that once you begin moving in a positive direction you may not want to stop.

To use a down-home example, let's say that the grass in your yard desperately needs cutting. You know once you have cut the grass the yard will look great and therefore give you pleasure. The problem is the pleasure the yard will give you once the grass has been cut is not enough to get you up from the Sunday paper. You also recall that the lawn mower is out of gas so you would have to get gas, get the mower out, fill it up, and then mow. Then you must clean the lawn mower and sweep or wash down the patio and sidewalk. By time you get done, you reason, you'll have missed the first inning of the Dodgers' game.

Now, here's a better way to go about this project. Instead of making cutting the grass your goal, which demands more time and effort than your are willing to give, make getting the gas your goal. In this way the task will only take ten minutes and then you will be ready to cut the grass next time you have a spare fifteen minutes. By cutting the time needed to accomplish your goal in half you have moved forward by getting in a position to achieve your goal. Without gas you can't move forward; by taking action now and getting gas you still have not cut the grass, but you are now in a position to do so. Often as you pour the gas into the lawn mower you might just find yourself ready to keep on going and take it out to the yard. The first inning of the game is seldom that good anyway. Plus when you are finished it will be afternoon and you won't feel bad about having a beer as a small reward. Get yourself to take action and both the little things and the big things will follow.

Rich DeVos, cofounder of Amway, said that people make very few big decisions in life. Rather, it's the string of small, seemingly insignificant decisions that usually makes the difference in the course of one's life. In his case, it was the simple decision to let another student, Jay Van Andel, share a ride to school in his Model A Ford for just 25 cents a week. Van Andel went on to become his business partner in creating one of the world's largest corporations.

TAKE ACTION EACH DAY THAT MOVES YOU CLOSER TO YOUR GOALS

Take some action each and every day that moves you closer to your goals and you will see your luck changing right before your eyes. If you want a new car just like your neighbors start putting away $10, $20, or $50 dollars a week. No matter what happens do not touch that money. If you need money, sell something, borrow it from a friend, or work overtime but do not touch the money you have put aside for your car. Very quickly you will find yourself "lucky" enough to have enough for a down payment.

If you want to lose twenty pounds start today by substituting a glass of water for one beer or can of soda. Walk up the stairs instead of taking the elevator. Eat half as much cereal for breakfast. Take a small step now that moves you closer to your goal. Follow it up with several more small steps and they'll soon add up. Before you know it you will find yourself halfway down the road to success.

I want you to think hard right now. What three actions could you take in the next ten or twenty minutes to set yourself into motion in direct pursuit of your dreams?

1. _____

2. _____

3. _____

Don't wait until you are on the ropes physically, mentally, or emotionally before you take action. Start now! Get out your list of goals, pick one, and start working toward it.

Some people find it easy to take action on one front that they particularly enjoy but then sabotage their chances for success by failing to take any action in another area that may be more important but that they do not find of any interest. For example, in a small business the owner often knows a great deal about the products she sells, but seldom knows much about advertising, marketing, and finance. She will go to great lengths to find out more about her products and be of service to her customers, yet she will never improve her advertising or marketing knowledge. This is one of the main reasons why 90 percent of all small businesses fail.

You must take action across the board in order to get where you want to go, whether it be in your business or in your personal life. You can't just take action on the things you like to do or that are easy; you also have to face the other things with equal vigor.

GENERAL YOU

Have you ever gone to work and found that all the things you asked other people to do yesterday have still not been finished? In fact, no one has taken any action at all! Have you gone home and found the plumber still hasn't fixed the dripping sink and the kid up the street who usually cuts you grass is sick and so didn't show? Have you waited for a friend to pick you up because your car is in the shop only to find out two hours later that he didn't write it down and so has forgotten about you? In short, have you ever felt like you are a one-soldier army?

If you have, good! Because that's exactly what you are! You are the general, captain, lieutenant, and janitor of your very own one-soldier army. As general you are in charge of all aspects of waging the battle for the ultimate prize: success. In this battle you have total responsibility for the success or failure of your campaign. You also have total responsibility for yourself and the troops who have placed their trust in you—your family and friends.

Imagine yourself as general. In fact, say out loud right now the word "general" and insert your last name after it. General Smith, General Jones, or whatever your surname happens to be. Repeat it right now slowly in a loud, commanding voice to yourself. Sounds good, doesn't it? Sounds like you have power and authority just because of the word general in front of your name. You are in charge and can take the action needed to accomplish whatever goals and objectives you have set.

You can attack the hill and charge to the top or you can gather your troops together and retreat to the beach, hoping the boats will still be there to pick you up. You can wait for recon to gather more reports in order to gauge enemy strength. You can wait for the weather to change or for darkness to give way to dawn. But you can also use military intelligence to gather information, use the weather to your advantage, and equip your troops with night vision goggles to cut through the darkness. As general, whether you take action to move forward toward your goals or you retreat from them, all the ultimate decisions and actions in your very own one-soldier army are under your control.

As the General, you are in charge of all the aspects of running an army. Although your army is large and complex, managing it can be boiled down to just a few key areas. Remarkably, some of these areas bear striking resemblance to the areas you must take action in to be a success in life.

You are in charge of several specialized functions. All of these functions must be reported to you on a regular basis so that you know exactly where you stand. Let's take a look at each of these functions individually to see what their obligations are to the army as a whole.

Planning

The first action you must take in any military campaign is to plan. You must decided on an objective. You must gauge the strength of the adversary you face and then size up your own strengths and weaknesses. You must then plan a strategy of attack complete with the specific goals and objectives you must achieve. You need to set times and dates for the accomplishment of each task and objective. Then as each new objective is reached you must update your plans, review them, process new information, and seek out new targets. Can you imagine what would have happened if General Norman Schwartzkopf had shown up in the Gulf War with no plans or objectives?

There is a scene in the movie *Apocalypse Now* where in the heat of a jungle battle a young captain new in the area yells, "Who's in charge here?" A soldier close to him shows a look of horror as he exclaims, "Oh my god, I thought you were!" You have to know who's in charge and exactly what the objective is. Without planning the war is lost before the battle even begins. Planning is a very important task in your capacity as general; you must take action in this area before you try to race ahead. You do this by completing the lessons dealing with defining your goals section of your workbook and then by developing strategies to attain them. It is the first and most vital action you must take toward your success.

Intelligence

Sometimes you do not have all the necessary information or skills in order to carry out your plan. In this case use your intelligence forces to secure more knowledge. In order to come up with new tactics and strategies attend briefings with other generals to learn from their successes, mistakes, and counsel. Study battles that have been fought in the past so you can learn from them. And always be on the lookout for new ways to motivate your troops.

Personal Staff

Their job is to give the public a briefing on the war and keep public opinion on your side. They perform an advertising and marketing function for the general and the war as a whole. Without public opinion on your side, funds will soon be cut off from the war and you will have to return home vanquished. This function will also determine how your actions are viewed in regard to future commands and promotions. Without action in this area you will be passed over quickly by other more ambitious generals.

Operations

Operations is where most Generals enjoy being, down with their men in the heat of the battle working in the trenches. This is the daily routine of work that adds up to help you attain your objectives. This is the work part of the army: supplies, transporting troops, fighting, and so on.

Good generals know, however, that without equal attention to their other duties in planning, intelligence, and public relations they will fail long before they have the opportunity to fight.

The Army as a Whole

As you can see, every one of these functions has equal value to your overall success as a general. If you put too much emphasis on operations, you will fail because planning and intelligence are neglected. If you place your emphasis on intelligence but fail to watch operations you could be out of ammunition very quickly. Although the public's focus is on the actual battle, your staff behind the scenes puts in a lot more than a few days fighting in order to win the war. You can't focus all your efforts in one area and expect to reap results across the board. You must take action on a broad scale in order to achieve your objectives.

We have now looked at the broad scale of action you must take in order to live up to your potential, but what happens if the action you take fails to produce the desired results in your life? Like all good generals you simply go to plan B.

Always Have a Plan B

Why put your life on hold waiting to get a promotion? Why not strive for that move up but also invest in plan B. All good generals have one. In fact, the words "plan B" came from the famous German general Bismarck. As general of your own one-soldier army you should always have a plan B.

Why not start a small business of your own on the side? Start one that offers you additional income and furthers your career. Start a mail-order business or a weekend business that focuses on your hobby. Why not sell model planes or baseball cards at the local flea market. My good friend David Miller turned his flea market stall into a million dollar enterprise in just six years selling martial arts supplies. How? Because of his passion for the martial arts and his products.

Mail order still offers one of the greatest opportunities in the United States. In fact, as people get busier the market continues to grow. I know that I find myself buying a huge amount of books, videos, casual clothing, and gifts through the mail. You can start with almost nothing and quickly turn a profit. I founded a mail-order business selling information. It had just three products and grossed over $200,000 the first year. How do you do this? It's simple: Make a plan and take action. While you are taking action 90 percent of the world is in limbo. Every time you are taking action you are moving forward. The more directed and specific that action is the faster you will be moving.

Look into opportunities as a consultant because corporations are downsizing their staff and they increasingly find the need to bring in outside experts for help with major projects.

What is your plan B? What action will you take if your first plan stalls or fails?

BE A DOER, NOT A DREAMER

A vital part of reaching your goals is the ability to dream. Dreams get you going, but at some point you must trade in your dream for the dedication and hard work that will help you realize it.

From my own research I have found that 95 percent of the people who read books like this will do nothing with the information. In fact, people who read books dealing with the topic of success fall into one of five categories.

1. There is a percentage of people who feel they already knew everything in this program and so learned nothing. Of course, despite the fact that they already know all of the information they never put any of it into practice.

2. Some people will read this book then tell all their friends how great it was. Meanwhile any action they should have taken gets shelved along with the book.

3. Then there are the people who think the book is great and call me up three weeks later to say that they have since read five other books and listened to three audio programs, yet this book is still their favorite. Instead of rushing out to expand their knowledge, they should instead take some direct action in their own situation first. Then they can pursue further information.

4. Perhaps the largest percentage of people are well-meaning procrastinators. They will take action just as soon as their relatives leave or after Christmas is over. They will start as soon as they sell their present business or house. In reality there is always something in the way to prevent the pursuit of their goals.

5. Then at last there is that 5 percent who truly take action and move toward great things in life. They fill out their goals, identify the people they need to help them, and plan the actions they must take to succeed. They are the people who will soon rise to the top and make it big in America. I hope you are one of them! Please don't just read this book and say, "Oh yeah, that was good." Take a chance and make your dreams come true.

COLUMBUS TOOK A CHANCE: WHY DON'T YOU?

Often taking action in one direction or another means taking a chance and therefore risking failure. I constantly have people writing and calling me to share in their new and wonderful ideas. They have found a niche, invented a widget, or got a great deal on a company they think will be big. Many of the ideas I listen to and read about make little sense, but a great many others sound exactly like wonderful opportunities just waiting to blossom. What a shame that so few of these ideas will ever make it past the idea stage and into reality.

Five hundred years ago a little-known sailor talked the queen of Spain into fronting the money for a trip to the end of the world. He was trying to discover a new and faster trade route to India. In taking the chance and by failing in his original mission by several thousand miles Christopher Columbus became the first man to make it big in America. Columbus took a chance, why don't you? The rewards are great and armed with the information and strategies this book provides the risks are few.

List the five main actions in your life you have been putting off that can help you move toward your goals (for example, getting more training, changing jobs, or finding an investor).

1. _____
2. _____
3. _____
4. _____
5. _____

List five reasons why you are putting off these actions.

1. _____
2. _____
3. _____
4. _____
5. _____

How can you change these reasons in order to get yourself to take action?

1. _____

2. _____

3. _____

4. _____

5. _____

Resolve now to take some kind of action each and every day, however little it seems to propel you toward your goals. As Yoda the Jedi Master in the *Star Wars* trilogy said, "Try? There is no *try*. There is only do or not do!"

LESSON 12

PERSISTENCE

Even though large tracts of Europe and many old and famous states have fallen or may fall into the grip of the Gestapo and all its odious apparatus of Nazi rule, we shall not flag or fail.

We shall go on to the end. We shall fight them in France; we shall fight on the seas and on the oceans; we shall fight with growing confidence and growing strength in the air; we shall defend our island, whatever the cost may be.

We shall fight on the beaches; we shall fight on the landing grounds; we shall fight in the fields and in the streets; we shall fight in the hills and we shall never surrender.

— WINSTON CHURCHILL

NEVER SURRENDER

Those immortal words were broadcast to the people of Britain on June 4, 1940, a week after the evacuation of three-quarters of a million men from Dunkirk on the coast of France. The rest of the countries in Europe had fallen with alarming speed at the hands of Hitler's war machine. The Nazis stood just outside of Paris and would soon be looking across the twenty miles of the English Channel toward London itself. At the time the fate of western Europe lay with the British. Despite the devastation of all the other armies in Europe and the seemingly hopeless odds Winston Churchill stood defiant in the face of the enemy. He believed that if he could hang on long enough something would happen that would change the course of the war in Britain's favor.

His bold persistence and indomitable spirit were the most important factors in the entire war. Many of the other cabinet ministers were later to say that without his constant encouragement and his dogged persistence Britain would never have held out until America entered the war and changed its course in the allies' favor.

Churchill has been described by many as the greatest man of the Twentieth Century and yet Churchill was far from successful in much of his early life. Despite flashes of brilliance and courage he faced more than the average share of disappointments and setbacks. He was hopeless at mathematics and had to take his military exam three times before being accepted into the military. Even then his scores were so poor that he had to go into the cavalry instead of the infantry as he had hoped.

Before reaching his post as prime minister he was defeated many times in local by-elections, losing his seat in Parliament, Britain's equivalent of the House of Representatives, not once but several times. After being removed from the position as First Lord of the Admiralty during the First World War after the loss of a battle he was quoted as saying to friends, "I am finished."

The difference was that after a few days to regroup he knew he was far from finished. He knew that no matter how bleak things looked at the moment greater days lay ahead for him. He knew that with patience and persistence his finest hour was yet to come!

THE POWER OF PERSISTENCE

This trait of persistence is found in all successful people
and is crucial to making it big. According to former President Calvin Coolidge, "Nothing takes the place of persistence," and if history is any judge he is certainly right.

Almost all of the world's great success stories are
drawn from the ashes of failure or despair. Remember our
look at the life of Lee Iacocca? He was fired by Ford only
to be made president of Chrysler and save it from total
ruin a matter of months after taking over. Later, Iacocca
became a national business hero and the ultimate proof
that success is the best revenge. History is full of generals
humiliated in battle returning to win the war's decisive
victory and of leaders like Lincoln and Churchill who on
the verge of utter despair could still summon the courage,
strength, and persistence to move entire nations to victory
when none seemed possible.

Persistence is the one final ingredient that truly separates those at the top from the also-ran's and wanna-be's.
Like all the other ingredients to success it is a simple one to
learn and putting it into action is as easy as deciding to
simply do it. This single ingredient of success has been mentioned and demonstrated by those at the top more than any
other factor. From Washington to Reagan and Edison to
Einstein this one lesson can be found in the biographies of
every person in the world who ever made it big.

THE SPIDER AND THE SCOTSMAN

An early demonstration of this quality is credited to a
Scottish warrior by the name of "Robert the Bruce," or
more accurately to a spider whose acquaintance he made.
Having fled from the oncoming armies prior to the battle

of Bannockburn, Robert was hiding in a cave tired, defeated, and depressed. He had failed, things had not gone as planned, and the future seemed hazy at best.

We have all been in a similar circumstance at one time and in some form or another, down and almost out for the count. Faced with bills, problems, and an uncertain future we hide in a cave of despair. What separates the winners from the losers in this world is whether they stay in the cave. It's easy to get up and go to work when things are going great; it's when things are not going well that the winners are separated from the losers.

After sleeping for several hours Robert woke up to see that a spider had spun a giant web that almost reached across the entire mouth of the cave. Before the spider could complete it's task a strong gust of wind blew the web to pieces. Undeterred the spider climbed back to the top of the cave and began its work again. Three times the wind howled through the cave and destroyed the web yet each time the spider climbed back to the top and started over.

Robert watched the spider for hours as it spun its web, searching his soul for answers to the seemingly insurmountable strength of his own enemy. Then after watching the spider's dogged determination Robert the Bruce saw the answer to his own problems, drawing strength from its strength of purpose. The following day he rounded up his weary men and lead them back into battle where they defeated the enemy despite being vastly outnumbered. The spider's message rings out today just as loud and clear as it did a few hundred years ago: If at first you don't succeed, try, try again.

ALL THE BEST PEOPLE FAIL

If you know a thing or two about baseball then you will probably already know the answer to this little piece of trivia. If you don't know much about baseball, the answer may surprise you. Who had the most strikeouts in baseball history?

The answer is Babe Ruth. Think about that: the game's all-time legend failed to hit the ball more times than any other player in history—over 1300 strikeouts in all. Do you think that Babe Ruth ever looked at his record that way? Of course not, he saw himself as the living legend; he was the home run king. Yet had he not stood at the plate as many times as he did, he would never have achieved the same degree of success. Your chances of success improve each and every time you step up to the plate.

Professional golf offers another great example. In the period between 1960 and 1986, Jack Nicklaus won an unprecedented twenty major golf championships. Wonderful though that is, it also means that he failed to win over 80 percent of the time.

Frederick Forsyth, author of many brilliant books, had his first book, *Day of the Jackal,* returned to him with the comment "No reader interest." It has now sold over ten million copies.

THE TURNING POINT TO GREATNESS

Before Rich DeVos and Jay Van Andel struck diamonds with Amway they sold products for Nutralite, a California company that marketed products through direct sales in much the same way as Amway would later do. Shortly after they got involved selling the products they held a big meeting to get distributors. They ran radio ads, newspaper ads, handed out flyers, and scoured the town telling everyone about the meeting. They were sure that the hall would be filled to capacity with people eager to hear what they had to say. That night despite their huge promotional effort only two people sat in the room set up for several hundred people. They gave their sales pitch as best they could to these two people and then drove home that night because they couldn't afford a motel room. When he later looked back on this evening DeVos laughed at the incident and said, "We could have done one of two things: either we could give up, or we could persist. We persisted." Later when Amway became a billion dollar corporation they bought the Nutralite company they had once represented. It is truly amazing how many turning points in people's lives come down to this simple decision: Should I try again or should I throw in the towel and resign myself to life as it is?

Why continue to struggle? After all, aren't there millions of people who are happy and content with their lives as they are? What's wrong with drawing a paycheck and not making a fuss—just going in to work at nine and leaving at five? What's the harm in taking evenings off to watch television and spending the weekends at the beach in the summer? Sure it would have been nice to have bought that condo in Aspen and that white Mercedes convertible, but we gave it our best shot once and it just didn't work. It would be nice to help out the poor people in town but we just don't have that much ourselves. Isn't it better to stay here in our little cave of comfort than to get up and try again?

Where would America be now if Lincoln, who had been defeated over eight times when running for public office, had thrown in the towel after any of his defeats?

Would you accept public defeat and indifference eight times and keep going? I hope so, because I have some news for you. If reading this book has interested you in getting ahead in your present job or starting a new business—get ready. If you have not yet incurred any setbacks in your life be prepared to handle them. As sure as the rewards of success are great, so are the obstacles that present themselves along the way. And they will present themselves on your road to the top. If you are prepared to try only once don't waste your time, effort, and money. Go out and buy yourself a new big-screen TV, because watching soap operas will do you almost as much good as trying only once to succeed. You must develop the trait of persistence and develop it soon.

How to Develop Persistence

The best way to develop persistence is to simply realize in advance that things do not always work out as you would like or expect them to in the short run. However, in the long run and with enough effort and energy invested in the right direction they almost always do. By understanding that failure and setbacks are not only possible but probable, you will be much more ready to deal with them when they occur. That having been said, you can increase your reserves of persistence instantly by not setting yourself up to fail.

Do Not Set Yourself Up for Failure

What do you mean, don't set myself up for failure? Why would I set myself up to fail? Is that what you're thinking? Well, the fact is people do set themselves up to fail because they have not moved past Lesson One and conquered their mental limitations about reaching the top. Others do it through a lack of thought and poor planning. Let me give you two examples. Do not go on a diet and then set up a meeting in your favorite French bakery full of chocolate eclairs, Napoleons, and fresh cream cakes. Do not resolve to cut down on drinking alcohol and then arrange to a meet a friend in your favorite bar the same evening. Do you see what I mean by setting yourself up for failure? These are perfect examples. By doing so you test your reserves of persistence in unnecessary ways.

Another way to set yourself up for failure is to place unrealistic time frames on what you wish to accomplish. This once again predisposes you for failure and tests your reserves of persistence more often than they should be tested. Your persistence should be tested only when outside forces beyond your control cause you to miss goals or deadlines. Making yourself fail because you have unrealistic target dates not only sets you up for failure but it also causes undue stress in your life. Notice I said *undue* stress. Let's take time out here for a second and discuss stress and its place in helping you get ahead.

Pass the Stress Test

You hear a lot about stress these days and how it can negatively affect relationships and health. But what is stress? Stress exists primarily in the mind: you create it and bring it on yourself by putting pressure on yourself. Not all forms of stress are bad; some stress can be good.

I put pressure on myself to work long hours and get projects finished. I do not have to do that, but I choose to do it because it helps me produce more work. The very first home I ever bought cost over $400,000 at a time when the average American home cost just $80,000. That put a lot of financial pressure on me to perform. Did I have to do that? Of course not, I could have paid cash for a two-bedroom condo or could have bought a nice home in a nearby area for half that price. I created my own pressure and stress but it was positive stress. By choosing to live in a very exclusive area I met a great many successful people whose ideas have been invaluable over the course of the years. I put myself on the edge so that I tried harder to perform, but had I taken on an even more expensive home I would have been putting so much pressure and stress on myself that the results would probably have been negative. This would have resulted in failure.

When the Spanish explorer Cortez landed at Vera-
cruz, the first thing he did was burn his ships. Then he
told his men, "You can either fight or die." Burning the
ships removed the third choice of returning to Spain. This
put pressure on his men to perform.

Now, do not put such severe pressure on yourself. Set
your goals and time frames high but not so high as to be
unreasonable. You must leave time in your planning for
unseen events: the copier breaks down, the computer
bombs, or a key associate is out sick with the flu for a
week. These are all things that happen in everyday life
and if your plans call for a project to be finished by the
end of the week they may well be thrown off. If your goal
is to make a million dollars this year that's fine, but if you
don't have a workable plan do not be too disappointed if
you fail to reach that goal. A much better goal might be to
make $250,000 this year and work up to a million over
the next five years. Having said that, however, I'll be the
first to admit that some people have such undying faith
and persistence that even seemingly impossible goals become possible. These people can visualize reaching their
goals.

Visualize Your Goals

Top athletes have known about the power of visualization
for years. Golfers and tennis, basketball, baseball, and
football players have all learned the usefulness of visualization in producing peak performance. And peak performance is the only kind of performance you should be
interested in because it's the only kind that quickly moves
you to your goals.

The ability to visualize the outcome of your goals is
critical to helping you reach them quickly. It is also critical in helping you build reserves of determination and persistence. The sharper and more vivid your vision the

easier it will be to accept defeat in one battle but still go on to win the war.

You must develop in your mind a picture of you as you will be when your goals have been reached. The respect you'll receive, your sense of achievement, and the house, car, vacations, and loving relationships you will enjoy when you reach your goals should all be part of your mental image. To you, this vision should be as vivid as the big screen TV in your family room. The sounds of victory should ring in your mind as loud as the cheers on Super Bowl Sunday.

How will you feel when you have all the success and respect that you deserve? What will you do with the money? Where will you go? How will you help others? Make sure the only movie that ever plays in your mind is *The Road to the Top* starring *you!*

Gary Player's most vivid memory of the 1965 U.S. Open, where he became the first non-American winner in over forty-five years, was something no one else could see. At the top of the giant scoreboard that listed all of the past winners was the name of the 1964 champion Ken Venturi. Yet right above his name in huge bold letters before the tournament even started was another name. It was the name of the 1965 champion, Gary Player. Said Player, "Make no mistake about it, the name on top of that board was mine." The power of visualization works, so use it to your advantage.

AN ALL-AMERICAN EXAMPLE OF PERSISTENCE

Back in the early seventies a young unknown screenwriter decided that he wanted to be an actor. He wrote himself a part in one of his own movie scripts. Like so many other writers and wanna-be movie stars he thought it was a good script. He also thought that he would be the perfect person to play not just a minor role but the starring role. Imagine a unheard of actor playing the lead role in a movie he also wrote.

He took his script around to many different people in Hollywood. Some told him that sports movies never made any money, others just wished him luck and showed him the door. The door was a lot further than he got with some of the rest. Still the young man kept trying to convince people that what he had was good material.

Finally after many months one studio offered to buy his script for what at the time must have seemed like a very large amount of money. Most people would have jumped at the chance just to have their screenplay turned in to a movie let alone getting paid handsomely for the privilege. But this young man had other ideas. He didn't just want to get paid for writing the script, he wanted to star in the movie. The studio made him a second offer. They offered him extra money if he would give up the ridiculous idea of starring in the movie and let a real star take the leading role.

He continued to struggle, with his wife working in a diner to make ends meet. He sold everything he had and put it all into making his movie. Finally, he scraped and borrowed enough money to make his dream a reality. Not only did this nobody win an Academy Award for the year's best screenplay, but his movie made over $100 million. Since then Sylvester Stallone's movies featuring Rocky Balboa and Rambo have grossed over $1.6 billion.

Stallone did not trust luck or fate to make him a movie star. He made himself a star and a household name because he believed in what he was doing and he let nothing stand between him and success. He set goals, made a plan, and took action to live his dreams. Every person that turned him down became one less person he needed to waste his time on. When faced with the partial success of selling his screenplay he turned it down and continued striving toward his real goal. In return for a burning belief in himself and unrelenting persistence he has been rewarded at the highest level.

This sort of persistence can and will work for you; the problem is that so few people possess persistence at anything but a rudimentary level. They try something once, twice, or maybe even three times and then quit. Remember the old saying "quitters never win and winners never quit"? Well it's true. Resolve to persevere in every goal, task, and action you undertake. Treat each setback as an example of another way not to reach the top. In this way you can view your setbacks as successes. You will waste no more time doing things in this particular way. Instead you will regroup and try a different approach.

EXPERIENCE AND WHAT TO DO WITH IT

"Experience is what you get when you are looking for something else." That's an interesting quote I read as a child on the back of a matchbox. I quoted it widely whenever anyone told me what a great experience playing a certain golf course or tournament was even if you played like a dog. Gaining experience in a nutshell is often very disappointing.

Professional sports offer a good look at the experience factor. In the Super Bowl each year the two best teams in the world come together on one Sunday afternoon in January. One will lose and will be faced with two options: They can quit and admit that they simply are not good enough to achieve the pinnacle of success or they can chalk it up to experience and try again next year. They of course opt for experience and try again.

Many people can tell you a story about a failed business venture that they had to chalk up to experience but I don't know a single person who ever set out with the goal of getting that experience. More likely they hoped to get rich quickly, then when it didn't happen quite that way they began instead to talk about the experience they got as if that was what they were after all along. There is, of course, absolutely nothing wrong with gaining experience even in this way. Experience is a fine thing to have as long as in the process of gaining that experience you truly learn something to prevent your getting the same result next time.

Many of the giants of this century as well as through-out history have experienced failure many times over. What separated them from the mass of humanity was that these great people viewed their failures as Edison did his, a success in how not to accomplish a particular task. They thereby eliminated another idea that did not work so that the path to success was clearer. This is a classic example of reframing at work as we discussed in Lesson Nine.

Presidential Experience

Former President Ronald Reagan in his autobiography talks of the small things in his life that proved to be turn-ing points. A particular turning point for him was apply-ing for a job as head of the sports department at a new Montgomery Ward store. They were looking for a local high school sports star and as Reagan had been a football star he was convinced that he would get the job. Fortu-nately for him he lost out to another local sports celebrity. This was a bitter disappointment to the young Reagan.

This small failure set him out looking to get into radio and so he traveled to Chicago. He dreamed of being a sports announcer but was turned down by every single station at which he applied. He did, however, leave with some good advice. He was told to start off by trying a smaller station in one of the more rural areas.

Discouraged but determined Reagan set off again in search of a job in broadcasting, this time at a smaller station. Within a few weeks he landed a job because he took action and continued to take action until he reached his goal.

Once at the station things did not go all that well and he was soon told that he would be replaced. This, of course, came as another bitter disappointment. Fortunately, the radio station asked him to stay on for a few days and help out his replacement. Instead of indignantly refusing as many others might have done Reagan agreed. Before the end of the week the person hired to replace him had decided not to accept the job and Reagan was asked to stay on until another replacement was found. He again agreed to do this but only under the condition that the station's most experienced person would spend time with him each day explaining what he had done wrong and how he could do better in the future so that he might find work with another station. This they did and as often happens when people seek out good advice Reagan was able to improve his performance so rapidly that the station stopped looking for a replacement. This is a perfect example of how to handle rejection and what you must do to ensure that this doesn't happen again.

DO NOT TAKE REJECTION PERSONALLY

One reason so many people never learn to become persistent is because they take every rejection, setback, or failure personally. They somehow equate their idea or product with their self-esteem and self-worth. In this type of negative thinking each failure in business means to these people that they are failures and losers in life and will never get ahead. Think back over past setbacks, are they really a reflection on you as a person? Of course not.

TREAT YOURSELF THE WAY YOU TREAT YOUR FRIENDS

If people were to treat their friends the same way they treat themselves when they encounter failure they simply wouldn't have any friends. You know what I mean, think back to a time where you experienced a setback and blamed it on yourself. I bet you said something like this to yourself: "You stupid moron you knew this might not work. How could anyone be so dumb to waste money in this way? What's the matter with you? You must be an idiot to ever get into this. You're such a fool."

Imagine talking to your friends like this—do you think that you would get a very positive reaction? Do you think you would keep your friends very long? No way! After one or two lines they are going to tell you exactly where to go with your abuse. By beating yourself up over setbacks you will not generate a positive reaction from your own mind or body any more than you would from a friend.

Get out of the habit of beating yourself up mentally when things go wrong. There are plenty of other people out there in the world willing to do it for you and they won't even charge. By focusing on blaming yourself you are breaking down your level of persistence and resolve. Sure, analyze what went wrong but don't take the rap personally even if it was your fault. Simply focus on a new angle of attack and use your mental energy to come up with a new solution. Remember, the past does not reflect what must happen in the future.

DON'T BEAT YOUR HEAD AGAINST THE WALL

To analyze what has gone wrong in the past and then change things so that it does not reoccur in the future it is necessary to possess another key trait, common sense.

Unfortunately, as my father Andrew Wood Flockhart is fond of quoting from Voltaire, "There is nothing common about common sense." Successful people surveyed by Gallup placed common sense above every other trait with the exception of hard work. Intelligence, often quoted by many as a prerequisite for success, placed far lower on the list. Being persistent does not mean ignorantly smashing your head against a brick wall. Doing the same thing poorly over and over again is unlikely to produce the desired results.

After each setback you must sit down and try to refine your approach. First, when analyzing why things went wrong use only facts not fiction. Many times we are ready to jump to conclusions to rationalize our failure. One way to avoid this is to ask yourself, "How do I know this is true?" Often when that question is posed you'll find that it is not true and must then look for the real reason why you were rejected.

Look at your timing, was it good? Look at your marketing and your sales approach. Look at all aspects of your project and clearly define why your plans did not work out the way you wanted. If you can't discover why you were rejected solicit the help of those who rejected you. Ask them why they turned you down. Then ask them how you could change your approach to interest them or others in you or your products.

Most people love it when you ask for their opinion and love it even more when you call on them to help you. It gives them a feeling of power and importance. Use their feedback to refine your approach and then give it another shot. After each attempt take stock of the feedback and modify your approach accordingly.

Once you have modified your approach to the problem at hand remember the spider and the Scotsman and try again, and again, and again. It is always too soon to quit if you are in pursuit of a worthy goal.

If you have suffered a setback or failed to reach a goal do you know why? List the five major reasons below.

1. _____
2. _____
3. _____
4. _____
5. _____

Now list five major things you will never achieve if you quit trying now.

1. _____
2. _____
3. _____
4. _____
5. _____

REMEMBER YOUR DREAMS

Look very carefully at the five things you will never achieve if you quit: Aren't they worth giving it one more shot? Of course they are, and if it still doesn't work your goals and dreams are worth yet another shot after that. When you find yourself facing major problems go back and look at your list of goals. Clear your mind of all other things and remind yourself how it's going to feel swimming alongside that chartered yacht off the coast of Tahiti. Think how great it will be when you have no financial worries in your life and have a beautiful vacation home in Colorado. Imagine all the people you can help to lead better lives when you have taken care of your own needs.

Look at each of your goals one by one and visualize how you are going to think and feel when you have realized them. As you did before, visualize the sights, hear the sounds, and smell the sweet smell of success. Now that you are in touch with all those wonderful things go back and follow the steps in Lesson Nine to solve your present problems. As soon as you have done that you will have demonstrated persistence and following on from there is not hard at all. Remember the song "Rat Trap" I mentioned in Lesson Ten? The lyrics were "you can make it if you want to or you need it bad enough." It's up to you: persistence is a simple case of taking action again and again until you reach your goals.

It is as easy as saying, "Let's do it!" You are in charge of your own life; you are the one who has to make things happen. So what if they didn't happen this time. Sure it's a setback and a little hard to swallow. Your pride has taken a hit, your ego is a little deflated, and maybe people are saying "I told you so!" But remember they also said that before airplanes could fly. They said that when light bulbs didn't illuminate. They said that when someone suggested that man could land on the moon and the first rocket blew up on the launch pad. Yes many people more impressive and famous than you have faced setbacks, failures, and even out-and-out disasters. Mentally, physically, and emotionally they have been where you are now; all you have to do is get up and try again. The simple act of doing this will one day give you the right to join these people, all of whom were just ordinary people until they picked themselves up that one extra time that lead to greatness.

THE FROGS' LESSON

During a cold and stormy night two frogs found their way into a dairy through a hole in the floor. Once inside they began to explore the place and soon came upon a large stainless steel bucket full of cream. Jumping up to get a better look they landed in the bucket.

Both frogs tried valiantly to get out but they could get no footing. The first frog, after splashing and kicking for a few minutes, decided that the situation was hopeless so he gave up and drowned. The second frog persisted splashing and kicking for hours. His limbs were at the point of exhaustion and he, too, felt like giving up but he vowed to continue to the end. As dawn grew near his continual kicking finally turned the cream into butter whereupon he found enough footing to leap out to safety.

The story is simple and the lesson is clear. Give it one more try! And then another and another! The great thing about the game of life is that your are the umpire, referee, judge, and jury. Only you decide when you have struck out. In life you don't just get three swings at the ball. You can have three hundred or even three thousand—it is entirely up to you! The more swings you take the more chances you have to hit a home run. Sure some of those curve balls are going to end up as misses that might even make you look foolish, but just wipe off your hands and get back up to the plate. You'll eventually hit a home run.

Only you can sentence your dreams to death just as only you can pick yourself up and reach for them again. I can assure you that your dreams are worth every bit of effort and persistence you can muster. There is no better feeling in life than to live your dream. Go for it!

Well, we've reached the end of my book, haven't we. But it's only the beginning of a new and more wonderful life for you. Return to this book again and again; I guarantee you'll find something new and useful every time you read it. Use this book to plan your attack, then go after your dreams with passion and vigor.

By the way, I would love to know how you are doing in the pursuit of your goals, so why not write and tell me? Write to me in care of the publisher.

Resolve to develop and maintain the persistence to make your dreams come true!

INDEX